Piddington's Secrets

Martin T Hart

AKA

The Manipulatist

Editor

Caroline Kafka

First Published in 2015

ISBN: 978-0-578-15579-1

MANIPULATIST BOOKS GLOBAL
London ~ San Francisco ~ Shenyang

DEDICATION

This book is dedicated to the memory of my Mother, Eileen Beatrice Hart, who had a magical presence, a nurturing nature and the mind of a genius. Mum always knew what to say in any situation. When I was a young 18 years old, my then girlfriend and I sat down and confessed that we were having a baby. Expecting a wrath of disapproval she simply said; "it's not the end of the world, it's the beginning." Then, in 2013, my 17 year old daughter confessed to me she was pregnant and I began my shocked reaction with my mother's words "it's not the end of the world, it's the beginning." I miss her very much and will always treasure her last piece of advice to me; "Keep your nose to the grindstone" she said, meaning that if I work hard at what I want to do in life, I shall inevitably succeed. I pass her advice forward to all who have a dream. When you have success because you did not give up or through your own hard work, that's the Eileen Hart effect!

ACKNOWLEDGMENTS

Jesse Cox (Grandson of Sydney Piddington & Lesley Pope)
News.bbc.co.uk
the Spectator's Notebook section: 20th January 1950 (Page 5)
Archive.spectator.co.uk
Australian War Memorial (AWM)
the Railway Man (ISBN 0-09-958231-7)
Barry Wiley CD
Nigel Starck
National Library Magazine
ABC / 2UE Radio
Robyn Piddington (Nee Greig)
ThePiddingtons.com / Russell Braddon
Paul Daniels
Zoe Beloff (Daughter of John Beloff)
Keith's Korner.wordpress.com
Radio Lab
Wikipedia.org

Added Support

Bill Davenport: DavenportsMagic.co.uk
Joe Pon: Misdirections.com
Deng Fang (MBG.SF Publishing America)
Zhu Dipeng (MBG.SY Publishing China)

Photographs

Central Line Tube Sign (ThePiddingtons.com)
Ian Messiter (ThePiddingtons.com)
Lesley Concentrates (ThePiddingtons.com)
Ration Card Sample (Public Domain)
Green Pound Note Sample (Public Domain)
Dudley Perkins (SJ) (ThePiddingtons.com)
Rachel Hart Envelope Pass (ThePiddingtons.com)
Lesley Pope on board (ThePiddingtons.com)
Sydney & Gladys at the Mic (ThePiddingtons.com)
Lesley happy to receive poem (ThePiddingtons.com)
News Photo Lesley in Diving Bell (ThePiddingtons.com)
Stanley Mearns (ThePiddingtons.com)
Rosamund John (ThePiddingtons.com)
Noel Langley (ThePiddingtons.com)
Abacus 6 & 3 (Manipulatist Books)
Life of Ben Disraeli Book Line (ThePiddingtons.com)
Lionel Hale (ThePiddingtons.com)
Duncan Carse (ThePiddingtons.com)
Edana Romney (ThePiddingtons.com)
STRIKE (Manipulatist Books)
Jack of Diamonds (Manip Studios)

Piddingtons at London home (ThePiddingtons.com)
Dennis Price (ThePiddingtons.com)
Zener Cards (ThePiddingtons.com)
Hubert Pearce ESP (ThePiddingtons.com)
Changi POWs (ThePiddingtons.com)
Piddingtons 1947 (ThePiddingtons.com)
Piddingtons Hyde Park 1949 (ThePiddingtons.com)
Blindfolded Man (Public Domain)
Piccadilly Studio (ThePiddingtons.com)
U.S army typed letter 1 & 2
Fingers Crossed (ThePiddingtons.com)
Sketches by Ronald Searle (ThePiddingtons.com)
Nails (ThePiddingtons.com)
Stratocruiser (ThePiddingtons.com)
Hugh Williams (ThePiddingtons.com)
Derrick De Marney (ThePiddingtons.com)
Gladys Young (ThePiddingtons.com)
Dudley Perkins (ThePiddingtons.com)
At the Mic Steven Grenfell (ThePiddingtons.com)
Abacus Number 10 (Manipulatist Books)
Page Number Force (ThePiddingtons.com)
Piddington's Line Check (ThePiddingtons.com)
Cruickshank Sketch (ThePiddingtons.com)
John Beloff (Zoe Beloff - 'Family')
Piddington's Poster (ThePiddingtons.com)
RAF Writing Pad & Excerpts (Hart Family Album)
Sydney Piddington (ThePiddingtons.com)

Witnesses
George Hart
Rachel Hart
Brian Hart Senior
David Daye
Bridie Daye
Dicki Cole
Vivian Goldstein

Model
Georgia Eileen Hart

Historic Researchers
Lionel Hale
Nigel Starck
Barry Wiley

Investigative Research
Martin T Hart
Brian Hart Senior

CONTENTS

"Of course, if I had a grandson who wanted to carry it on, I would have enormous difficulty telling him how to. I don't think it would be possible, because there is an awful lot that I wouldn't be able to tell you, it's hard to explain why I wouldn't be able to. It's just that I wouldn't be able to."

Lesley (Pope) Piddington to her grandson Jesse
Page 56 and 57

"Here it is, you are the Judge"

Sydney George Piddington

SINCERITY CONTRACT

I, ________________________________,

as a member and practitioner of 21st century magic, promise that I will NEVER lend, give or sell this book to anyone, nor will I ever share the secret methods described herein. I make this pledge out of veneration to our industry and to the memory of the Piddingtons, whose wishes for confidentiality I respect.

Signed: ____________________________

Date: _________ / _________ / _________

Sign, Date, Photograph and Email to
Promise@ThePiddingtons.com

Your sincerity contract can be displayed on the dedicated website gallery-of-promises page

Hear their BBC Radio broadcasts online at:

ThePiddingtons.com

A great way to enjoy this book is to listen to the surviving BBC radio broadcasts available at the above website address. Afterwards visit the chapter on the broadcast you have heard to peek behind the scenes at what was really going on in the Piccadilly studios. Each recording hides a different story, even if some of the methods have been used more than once.

Once you know how each trick was achieved, listen again to hear the many events you had not noticed before, the mistakes that were made and the cunning way Sydney rescues himself from every situation. You will hear these broadcasts with new eyes, see with fresh ears and marvel at the talented geniuses the Piddingtons truly were.

Brian Hart (Senior)

PREFACE

. . .

Wow what a journey! Have you ever tried to write a book? I can tell you it is the most amazing journey a person can undertake, especially if the book is about real life events or about a person who truly existed. My journey has been packed with revelation, inspiration and perspiration. Piddington's Secrets has been in the making for an incredible seventeen years, beginning in 1998, seven years after Sydney Piddington passed away.

I know this may sound absolutely ridiculous but the events leading up to this book seem almost divine. I am not suggesting that the ghost of Sydney Piddington somehow steered this book into existence but it sure feels that way.

He was adamant in life, and rightly so, that his methods be kept secret, that no other magician should be allowed to perform his inventions or adapt his systems for improved or bigger telepathy effects. I suspect the spark for his act was a contributing factor in this. He was in the Changi POW camp suffering the hell of hunger, weakness and the fear of death. The idea to create his act came accidentally through a chain of events that ended with him reading a stray copy of the Reader's Digest magazine, in which, happened to be an article on Extra Sensory Perception. The effort that went into devising his methods in a place where any future looked uncertain must have created a strong emotional attachment with his methods, the tricks being as refreshing as a water supply in a harsh and merciless desert.

My journey began back in 1998, when I was working as a producer and presenter. I had my own radio show in London called 'The People's Show'. I interviewed many celebrities for the series and this led to writing a book with British magician Paul Daniels on the subject of 'Con Games.' That's when my father mentioned that his father, my granddad, worked with Sydney Piddington back in 1949. It was just an 'off-the-cuff' comment.

Growing up, I remember hearing many stories about the old days from my extended family members, which included behind the scenes adventures with the Piddingtons. But at the time I did not make the connection that these memories were of Sydney and Lesley Piddington, this was because Sydney was referred to as 'Piddo' and the couple referred to as 'the Piddos.' That said I still had no idea of their importance until I began to research the name 'Piddington.' Even then I had no idea the methods had never been discovered. So you can see how slowly and how long it took me to really begin to realise what was trying to unfold.

I mentioned that it seemed like 'divine intervention,' because of the way I began to unravel this amazing piece of history. After my father's 'off-the-cuff' comment in 1998 I conversed with family members who told me more about my Grandfather's involvement in the Piddington's BBC broadcasts. At this time I was just curious, there was no intention of writing a book. Each time I stopped thinking about this story something else would come to my attention, usually coincidentally, that would cause my interest to awaken again. It could be a comment, seeing some mind-magic on television or when a boring quiet Sunday gave me time to hear my thoughts.

A visit to my elders was always magical. I would like to thank my Nan's brother who we called Uncle Dave for showing me the card tricks he had learned from Sydney, although he never revealed to me how they were done. However, his many stories about his adventures with the BBC shows and the social meetings he enjoyed with the 'Piddos' were fascinating. Uncle Dave has since died, but I am sure he is still baffling them all up in Heaven with his well-practiced card skills.

Uncle Dave's wife Bridie Daye deserves recognition for all the times we sat up overnight just talking about how the 'Piddos' devised their demonstrations and of the many funny and worrying events from behind the scenes. We spoke of life, love and shared our whines about the world.

I thank my Father for his help in searching our disorganised attic for all and anything from the Piddington days. I was hoping to find photos or letters but instead found my Grandfather's RAF notebook, containing the methods that allowed Sydney Piddington to produce the miracle of thought transference in the studio, on stage and even in a scientific test conducted back in the Changi POW camp. This was my biggest find and one I studied over and over again to really understand what I was being told by this now fragile notebook.

After a slow but fruitful 15 years of gathering information about the entwined events between my elders and the Piddingtons and the discovery of the RAF notebook I needed to find as many recordings of the shows that existed. I needed to see if I could actually hear the methods being used.

Like a well-timed divine hand out of the dark, I accidentally discovered Jesse Cox, Piddingtons grandson, a man with a keen interest in discovering the methods. It was only at this point I discovered that even the immediate Piddington family didn't know how it was all done.

Jesse had tried to discover the secrets by asking his grandmother Lesley to share the methods with him, but she refused to do so. Jesse wrote an award winning radio documentary about his quest, which ended in him remaining in the dark. This was when I had the idea of writing this book.

I contacted Jesse and told him I knew their methods and asked if he would allow me to write a book about them? He said I could. I thank Jesse for all his help and support, for sharing the BBC recordings with me and putting me in touch with others.

My research intensified as I contacted all I could find who had ever researched or met the Piddingtons.

Thank you to the talented Nigel Stark for his contribution to keeping the Piddingtons story fresh and the great Barry

Wiley for his close and personal insight to Sydney Piddington's life during his final years. I recommend Barry Wiley's CD documentary 'The Piddingtons' for the exclusive recordings of Sydney explaining his ideas and the remarkable insight into the journey the act took. A download version is available online.

Many thanks also must go to Sydney Piddington's second wife Robyn Piddington (nee Greig) who agreed to rummage through her stored memories for the original radio scripts.

There were times when I felt worry, mainly because I was revealing another magician's secrets, a man who never allowed his secrets revealed in his own lifetime. I often battled with my conscience asking myself, was I doing the right thing? Here was a manuscript designed to end a controversy that took Sydney a lifetime to create, methods that were born out of a desperate need to save lives by rescuing the POWs from thoughts of never going home. I would like to pay a special recognition to my dear sister, Jacqueline Hart who battled my demons with me over the final year of writing this book. I thank her for her support and encouragement and for allowing me to bore her silly with the same subject matter.

I would also like to thank both Joe Pon, owner of *Misdirections* magic store in San Francisco who made me feel so welcome, and Bill Davenport of the *Davenports* magic shop in London, for their encouragement, and for discussing with me the importance of passing down these methods to the magic industry, thus giving me further confirmation that I was indeed doing the right thing.

I thank my Father, Brian Hart, for being a great Dad, an inspirational part of my life and for always making me feel safe when I have felt so vulnerable. Thank you Dad, for being the guinea pig when I wanted to try out Sydney's cunning methods for myself by performing them privately to the family, and (ironically) for not revealing how I did it.

On the academic side, I would like to thank my editor Caroline Kafka for all her hard work, for her direction, ideas and dedication.

Finally I would like to thank you guys, the magicians, for all your kind and encouraging comments through ThePiddingtons.com website. Thanks for letting me know that this book was important to you, that you would value knowing how they did it after nearly 70 years of silence. In the words of the amazing James Randi, from an interview with Max Maven at the Magic Castle in Hollywood (January 16th 2012) he said, "Methods shared often come back much improved."

I have structured the book to allow you the freedom to jump around the chapters in an order of your own choosing, without missing-a-trick. I know you may want to race forward to seek out the methods that have baffled you, or jump ahead to a particular broadcast. However you choose to read the book, I am glad to share this history and hope you enjoy the incredible journey the amazing Piddingtons travelled.

INTRODUCTION

. . .

The Piddingtons caused a war of thoughts and opinions, engaging the interest of approximately 20 million listeners each week, a massive number of people, brains and conversations, theories, ideas, criticisms and controversies.

So how did they think it was done? Many believed the Piddingtons used contraptions of some description. Transmitters concealed in teeth, secret pulse devices hidden in the shoes and books that had all the same pages throughout. It was even suggested that Sydney Piddington's stammer was in fact a code similar to the famous Morse code. On some of the broadcasts people from the audience can be heard coughing and it was thought they were delivering a secret cough code. Of course this was not the case but in some of the broadcasts it is easy to see why such ideas were formed. During periods of silent concentration, coughs would be heard, and they do sound code-like to someone seeking to identify a code during such a silence.

The above ideas were not true so how was it possible to send a thought from one mind to another without any sign of cheating?

It is believed the Telepathist Sydney Piddington took his secrets to the grave. The methods behind his ability to transmit his thoughts to his wife Lesley, in complete silence, (thus kicking to one side any notion a spoken code was in use), and even while she was somewhere else in the country, (squashing any idea that a visual code was at work), were seemingly gone forever, leaving future generations of magicians, from all genres of the craft, baffled and disappointed.

However, this is not true! Sydney Piddington's amazing methods are indeed known - and for the very first time – they are detailed here in this long awaited book. Sydney Piddington did share his secrets with others, for example, the BBC producers who worked on his broadcasts knew of his methods in order that they could collude with the illusion. Meanwhile, outside of the BBC media engine that housed the Piddington broadcasts, and more secreted in his private life, were those others who knew of his methods, including a family of hard working London taxi-drivers, the Harts and their close relations, the Daye's also.

Others have also declared owning knowledge about the Piddington's secret, for example, on the 17th July 2012, author Barry Wiley wrote an online blog;

"Though an American, I knew Syd Piddington for the last 10-12 years of his life and, of course, his wonderful second wife, Robyn. I have lectured and written on The Piddingtons at the Magic Circle in London and at various venues in the U.S. We never discussed methods (I have copies of all the radio scripts which Syd gave me) as I wasn't interested in methods, I was only interested his experiences and how he framed the show from week to week. We met during one of my business trips to Australia and talked at length. I did a mindreading act in college so I was very familiar with mindreading methods and such when we talked. We also spent a good deal on telephone bills. Syd was a marvellous personality, a quick smile and a great laugh. I do know how some of the

Piddington events were done, but I have no intention of giving anything away.

Syd told me that, when challenged to be tested by the SPR, that they were already topping the bill at the Palladium, and getting an SPR endorsement would add nothing and do nothing for them. Syd signed and gave me a copy of their poster from their South African tour. Magicians at the time would apparently duplicate the Piddingtons, but it never fazed Syd and they would then refute the method on their next show. Syd's specialty when he was young before the War was cigarettes and whistling, not mindreading. The mindreading started in Changi.

The key thing is that the Piddingtons did their act silently. The information to be sent was not shown to Syd until after he stopped talking. That was the point that frustrated so many magicians and reporters. And what made everything so great!

The Piddingtons were the best two-person mental act of the 20th century". (Keep them guessing). (July 17th 2012 ABC.net.au 360-Documentaries).

My name is Martin Thomas Hart and I am a freelance investigative journalist. I began my career in the media by inventing a detective solving murder game called 'Alibis'. The reader could identify the 'whodunit' by establishing the facts of each alibi in the short story. From this, I began creating puzzles which were to be regularly published in a young adults magazine called 'Fast Forward Poster and Puzzler' with BBC Worldwide magazines

I went on to study radio journalism and worked with a jamboree of radio stations within the BBC, gaining experience in producing and presenting. I was soon riding the crest of the wave in the newsroom gathering contributors for stories and on occasion, chatting to some famous people. Within two years I was presenting my own show with help from, comedy movie legend, Sir Norman Wisdom, the late great Sir Harry Secombe and a sack full of other celebrities including one of the UK's most prolific magicians, Paul Daniels.

It was during this period when, during a normal conversation with my father, Brian Hart, whilst he was pointing out an error I made in an interview on the radio, he made a throwaway comment, about his father, George Hart.

At the time, my father was discussing that me working in radio was not unique to the family as his father, George Hart, helped a famous man on the radio once. This famous man, it transpired none other than Sydney Piddington. However, at the time, the comment was non-consequential, and I did not give it another thought until much later.

I have always been interested in magic and I like to perform mind blowing tricks to members of my family. The off-the-shelf tricks fool them quite successfully but my mentalism effects often have them begging for answers. Buying a trick or even just the method of a trick is so easy now-a-days. In a few clicks you can download tutorials or within a few days the postman is handing you the secrets on the front door step.

I always found that I had figured out how the trick was done before I received it in the post. I guess I just have a different eye when watching these illusions. This has encouraged me to create methods to achieve some of my own ideas. One day I may even get the chance to perform them, and if I do, I am confident they will be as baffling as Piddington's Secrets. Enough haughtiness, let's move on.

I was born in London in the year 1966, the year England won the world cup. I was raised a Catholic boy who was educated in a Catholic primary school through the 1970s. Later, I went to an all-boys secondary school and then onto college. When I left, I had no idea what I wanted to do for a career, so I started out as a care assistant in an elderly people's home.

I found this fascinating work. I was surrounded by people who had much to share, experiences; stories; a lifetime of other peoples' memories cocooned my attention span through the day. One elderly man showed me his magic tricks. He was very good at lighting cigarettes and making them vanish, only to reappear from his mouth or hands. I could not catch him using sleight of hand. His card tricks were baffling to me at the time and I liked him a lot. Coincidentally, his name was also Sydney.

However, with no real direction in life, one day I found myself in trouble with the police, nothing serious, I was stopped in the early hours of the morning walking the street returning home from a party. I thought it was clever to give them false details about my identity, but as I discovered, it wasn't clever at all. I was arrested to establish my true identity and questioned as to why I withheld it. This meant I had to spend the night in a police cell and that is where I created and performed my first magical illusion and it is where my life changed forever.

In the cold silent echoes of the cell, I felt very alone. I felt sorry for putting myself there and just like 'a near death experience' I suddenly looked at life in a new way.

I vowed I would never get into trouble again and as a Catholic I prayed to God to set me free from the cell. My mind was very young then and I began to imagine ways to escape the cell. This was the very first time I created an illusion. I knew I could not really escape from a locked police cell, so I would just have to give the illusion I had vanished.

I thought long and hard and looked around the cell in detail. It was obviously designed to be inescapable. I noticed the cell was separated into two areas. One was an area with a bench-come-bed, while the other was a toilet made private by a walled partition with no door. Each of these areas was viewable through a peep hole in both the wall and door of the cell. So how to give the illusion I had vanished? I could do it by using the points of view to mislead the custody officer whose job it was to peek at me every hour.

I had already been peeked at a couple of times so I knew already that the first peek was always through the peep hole on the cell door. I also knew that once I had been observed, the peep hole was closed and the officer satisfied. So what would happen if when he peeked through the door he found I was not there? Obviously he would move across to the peep hole in the wall of the toilet area and look through that one.

The two peep holes were about a door width apart, about 3 feet, so the officer could not look through both at the same time. Have you figured out the illusion I managed to create yet?

When I heard the officer making his rounds, I took up a position between the walls separating the two areas of the cell. This was thin so I had to have more of my body in the toilet area first. Once I heard the peep hole in the cell door open then close, I shuffled most of my body into the cell area, leaving the toilet area empty of me. This only took a second. Once I heard the peep hole in the toilet area open and close, I again shifted my position so I was not visible in the cell area. It appeared as if I was not in the cell anymore because he had not seen me in both areas of the cell. It was inevitable that the officer would alternate between the two peep holes rather than use the same one twice. Confused, the custody officer obtained keys from another officer and had to open the cell door. I waited to hear the keys enter the lock; I knew the peep hole would be closed as it always swung closed unless held. This sound was my cue and only opportunity to dash to the bench and lay down as if asleep. On entering the cell, the officer, although confused, was satisfied all was well and his prisoner had not vanished after all. He said nothing and backed out almost immediately locking the door again.

I knew he was confused because once the door was locked; he took a look through the peep hole again, obviously to check his own sanity. I smiled and decided this was my calling. Not being locked up, but creating illusion and magic, miracles and amazement. This was my new buzz and with the knowledge the old gentleman, Sydney had imparted to me, I had the beginnings of something that I hoped would become my legacy.

So here I am, but this is not my story. This is the story of a man who deserves his award for 'best kept secret' in mind magic. The world already knows that Sydney Piddington was a genius, and now the world is going to find out why.

Thus, I return to my father's comment about my grandfather working for Sydney Piddington.

Sydney met my Grandfather, George, in London, while travelling in a black taxi cab. My grandfather was the taxi-driver. Sydney was looking to engage a person who was skilled at remembering things, someone who could get to grips with a new system of knowledge he had invented during the Second World War. For Sydney, the perfect person for such a task would be a London black-taxi driver because such cab drivers had to learn a skill called 'The Knowledge' a compulsory component of the Black Cab Carriage Licence in London.

The 'Knowledge of London' or more commonly known as 'The Knowledge' was introduced in 1851 by Sir Richard Mayne following complaints regarding cab drivers who did not know where they were going. In order to pass the test, involves detailed recall of 25,000 streets within a six-mile radius of Charing Cross station. The locations of clubs, hospitals, hotels, railway stations, parks, theatres, courts, restaurants, colleges, government buildings and places of worship are also required. It can take three years to pass the test, including the six months it takes to be tested.

Sydney Piddington knew that if anyone could master his systems, a licensed London taxi driver could find his way around it. George did not know it, but Piddington had been scouting for the right man since his arrival. He could not bring his usual help with him from Australia. Piddington was also looking for a driver who had good mathematical skills and could also keep secrets and as George was not a talker like many other taxi drivers were, he fitted the bill very well. Therefore, George was hired by Sydney, though kept his day job as a Black Cab driver.

Grandfather George told his wife Rachel, my wonderful Nan, about the extra money and it wasn't long before both Sydney Piddington and his wife Lesley arranged to meet up at my Grandfather's home in Cricklewood, north-west London.

Everything I find out from here on comes from the memory of my father Brian who recalls all his conversations with his mother and father and his uncle Dave Daye, as they talked about their experiences a lot over the years. Also from other family members, namely Dad's cousins Roberta and Jacky and the children of Nan's sisters Kitty and Barbara. Furthermore, George Hart made notes about Piddington's methods in an RAF notebook, with the notes still in existence today.

The first thing Sydney did was request that both my Grandparents sign a confidentiality agreement preventing anyone talking about, or in any way revealing details to any person. This was typed out on a single sheet of paper. Research shows that using an assistant or two is professionally risky as if they are discovered or if they happen to reveal that they are part of your illusion, then this has the potential to lead to cancellation of shows. Therefore, in every case where a person works with a professional magician he must have a legally binding '*Confidentiality Agreement*.' This basically means that any participant used in such acts can never divulge any information regarding their participation or the act itself at any time now or in the future. The exception to the rule is when under oath in a court room. Doing so will mean a contracted person will have to cover all your losses as a result of the disclosure, which in a professional magicians' case is often a lifetimes' work. These are pretty high consequences and are taken very seriously in law

If you have ever wondered why a magician's assistant has never exposed a famous magician, it is because of the confidentiality contract. Accordingly, a non-disclosure agreement (NDA), also known as a confidentiality agreement (CA), confidential disclosure agreement (CDA), proprietary information agreement (PIA), or secrecy agreement, is a legal contract between at least two parties that outlines confidential material, knowledge, or information that the parties wish to share with one another for certain purposes, but wish to restrict access to by third parties, or to the public. It is a contract through which the parties agree *not* to disclose information covered by the agreement. An NDA creates a confidential relationship between the parties to protect any type of confidential and proprietary information or trade secrets. As such, an NDA protects non-public business information or the secrets behind the illusions.

Many working magicians have many secrets they wish to protect, especially as this is how a magician makes a living. Therefore, it is advisable that a magician has such an agreement with everyone who secrets are disclosed to. Once a magician dies, unfortunately, the agreement is no longer valid. Therefore, though my Grandparents, George and Rachel, signed such a confidentiality agreement, in light of Sydney Piddington's death, the agreement is no longer valid. To keep the secrets after death is another document altogether.

Thus, Sydney offered both my Grandfather, George and Nanny, Rachel a paid role in his new venture. Sydney would later also engage my Nan's brother, David Daye;

who was also a London taxi driver and ex RAF gunner. On one occasion my Nan's brother-in-law, Dicki Cole, another taxi-driver, was also recruited.

My Father, Brian Hart, was only 8 years old at the time when the Piddingtons had rehearsals in his home, but he still remembers them practicing in the living room. His memories involve a tall man wearing a white blindfold while his mother, Rachel, wrote words onto a blackboard behind him.

My Grandfather George broke one of Piddington's rules, and that was not to write anything down. He was advised to use a blackboard to write any necessary notes and then rub out the chalk markings, however, my grandfather also wrote notes in a notebook. Though I do not know for sure why my Grandfather broke this rule, I am guessing it is so he could refer to something he could see when he was out working in his Taxi. Later, these writings were stored in a wooden Gramophone cabinet and forgotten about over the years, to be discovered recently.

The Morality Wall

At the time of the now not so inconsequential comment from my father regarding the Piddington's, I had no idea who the Piddingtons were, let alone what they did on the radio. It was only after my research had begun that I then realised the true significance of my father's comment.

I used the internet to find out more about the Piddingtons only to discover that people were still baffled about how they did their tricks. I was amazed to hear radio pieces all about how no one has ever discovered their secrets, including an award winning documentary by Jesse Cox, who is Sydney and Lesley Piddington's Grandson, trying to discover their secrets. However, it was only after I heard a radio piece by world renowned magician Penn Jillette of 'Penn & Teller' fame, exposing the mechanics behind one of the Piddingtons biggest effects, only to get it completely wrong, did I realise that I was probably the only person left who actually knew the Piddington secrets! However, I found myself battling with my inner morality. Was it right to reveal someone else's secret, a secret they had kept for so long?

As my battle with my inner conscience raged on I decided to contact Piddington's Grandson, Jesse Cox, to ask his permission to write a book exposing the methods behind his Grandparent’s amazing telepathy act. I received Jesse’s blessing, with offers to listen to his archive audio recordings of the BBC radio shows. Sydney Piddington’s second wife, Robyn, agreed to hunt down the surviving radio scripts for my research.

With this support, my mind was now made up and it was obvious that people were ready to know the truth behind the Piddingtons.

Important Note;

I have NOT structured this book as you may expect, and for very good reason. I have explained each show in order of where methods were used at their strongest to deliver unfathomable results. Some methods were used more than once on different broadcasts, thus you will find that I have repeated an examination of how the tricks were achieved. However, there is always something new to learn through each broadcast due to Sydney's many attempts at improving his effects.

It is also important to understand Sydney's background, and his experiences, to grasp fully how his mind worked and where he found the ideas behind his methods. It is a fascinating journey!

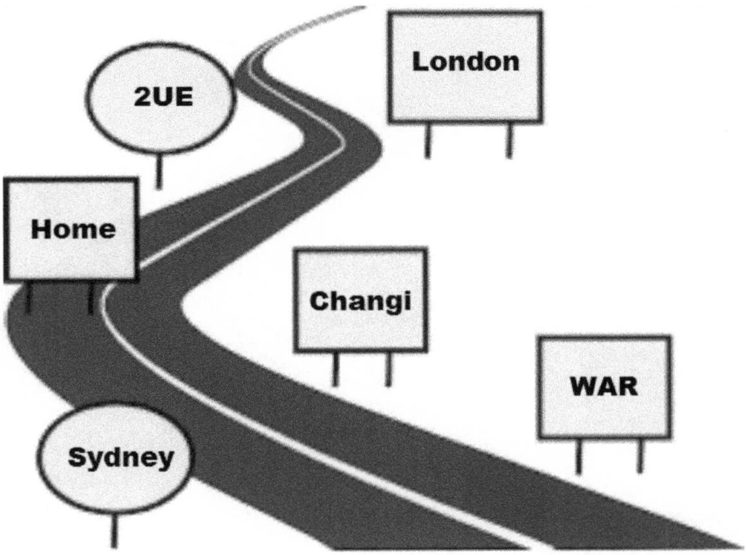

1 - THE PIDDINGTON'S

. . .

Sydney's story is well documented on the internet, mainly copied from the book, '*The Piddingtons*' by Russell Braddon published by Werner Laurie in March 1950 and a contribution authored for Wikipedia, the free online encyclopaedia. However, there are many more details in the Piddington story never published and I have inserted those missing details here, from reliable witnesses, Piddington's own words and an abyss of documentary evidence.

Far away from England, in an Australian city called Sydney, a little off to the side in the suburb of Randwick in New South Wales, Sydney Piddington was born on the 14th May 1918. Also on this day, the German and Lithuanian governments signed a Treaty of Alliance, which effectively placed Lithuania under German control, which ignited the chain of events that would later propel Sydney into war service.

Sydney Piddington grew tall and began his career in magic and mentalism in 1935 when, as a 17 year old amateur hobbyist, he joined the Independent Magical Performers of Sydney, the IMPS.

In those, his nursery years of magic, Sydney performed off-the-shelf tricks, usually with cards; he had not yet invented any methods of his own. And on the 1st of August 1936 his first real audience was seated at 'A Night of Magic' at the St James Hall in Sydney. Online website 'all-about-magicians.com' suggest that he performed the sleight of hand classic Cards To Pocket, brilliantly demonstrated by American conjurer Pop

Haydn on his 'You Tube' channel. Sydney also demonstrated the wonders of the Silk Jap Box, an empty wooden hand-held box where silks would appear inside of it, and vanish from its timbers. He performed a variety of classic magician's effects that he had learned from books and periodicals such as Jinx magazine and of course the inserted instruction sheets that came with each effect.

Sydney Piddington had a fascination with 'mind-magic' including the art of mind reading effects, mind control methods and, in particular, thought transference. Studying the work of American magician and inventor of mental and psychic conjurers' effects, Theodore Annemann, more commonly known as Ted, Piddington found his magical calling. Ted ran Jinx magazine and Syd often wrote to him.

The Psychic branch of magic, which adopted the idea that a strange phenomenon was at work, had already been around for a long time by the 1930s. Among magicians, the 'mentalism' performance that was cited as one of the earliest on record was by diplomat and pioneering, sleight-of-hand magician, Girolamo Scotto back in 1572.
With the onset of World War II, Sydney served in an artillery regiment in Singapore. Here there is a mammoth collection of stories depicting Piddington's many adventures during the conflict, stories of bravery, valour and determination. Such stories are brilliantly described by Braddon in his book, '*The Piddingtons*', However, what Braddon does not talk about is how methods of cunning used during missions involving Piddington were useful in his eventual telepathy act, instead, Braddon deliberately concealed the fact that Piddington's powers of extra sensory perception were just a trick. His book talks of real ESP tests, he quotes accuracy results and

quashes all and any attempts by the sceptics to reveal Piddington's methods, by pointing out how their ideas could not be right according to the controls implemented. Even in later interviews, Braddon continued to shy away from any suggestion that trickery was ever involved. Similarly, Piddington would talk about how he and Braddon experimented with thought transference for real, with never-a-mention of how they created any methods from which to fake the telepathy results. Many have reported that Braddon and Piddington created their 'methods' in the Changi POW camp, but neither of them have ever admitted to designing these.

After the fall of Singapore, Piddington was imprisoned for over 3 years in the Changi POW Camp. Fellow prisoners included Russell Braddon, who would later become an author of such works as 'The Naked Island' (1952), and sketch artist Ronald Searle, who drew illustrations of life in the Changi camp, and regiment Major Osmond Daltry, known as Ossie, were all close buddies in the camp. This friendship endured after their liberation. Braddon describes Changi as one of the more notorious Japanese Prisoner of War camps, used to imprison Malayan civilians and Allied soldiers. He says the treatment of POW's in Changi was harsh but fitting with the belief held by the Japanese Imperial Army that those who had surrendered to it were guilty of dishonouring their country and their families and, as such, deserved to be treated in no other way.

Entertainment in the camp came in the form of concerts put on by the prisoners themselves. Some of the prisoners were former actors, singers and musicians. It was relief from the harsh regime of forced labour and the onset of malnutrition, disease and fear of death.

There was a theatre built at one time but later closed when the Japanese guards took it away as a punishment. Braddon explains in an interview that the Japanese objected to one of the songs (On my return) that would be sung with gusto and pride during one of the performances. Piddington would perform his magic tricks for the men but as time ventured on, and 3 years had crawled by, the tricks were all but dry and so was much of the conversation. The men had all but told their life stories, their plans and dreams. It seemed all that could be said had been said. Apart from covert chat about what Piddington had heard on the BBC news, via a secret radio they had set up, there was little else to say. Moral was running as low as the rations, boredom was peeking high and Piddington, like the other prisoners, was soon reduced to merely surviving.

One day, after returning from forced labour, building a Japanese airfield, which ironically he would later open as a celebrity guest, Piddington stumbled across an article by Dr. J. B. Rhine on the subject of parapsychology. It was published in a stray copy of the Reader's Digest magazine he rescued from the dirt.

It was the most fulfilling read Piddington had had in years and he, once again, became enthralled by magic.

At the time, Doctor Joseph Banks Rhine was widely considered to be the "Father of Modern Parapsychology." Along with his wife Doctor Louis Rhine, he studied the phenomena now known as parapsychology at Duke University in Durham, North Carolina. Rhine collaborated with Professor William McDougall who served as the Chairman of the Department of Psychology. It was Rhine who coined the term "extrasensory perception" (ESP) to describe the apparent ability of some people to acquire information without the use of the known five senses. He also adopted the term "para-psychology" to distinguish his interests from mainstream psychology.

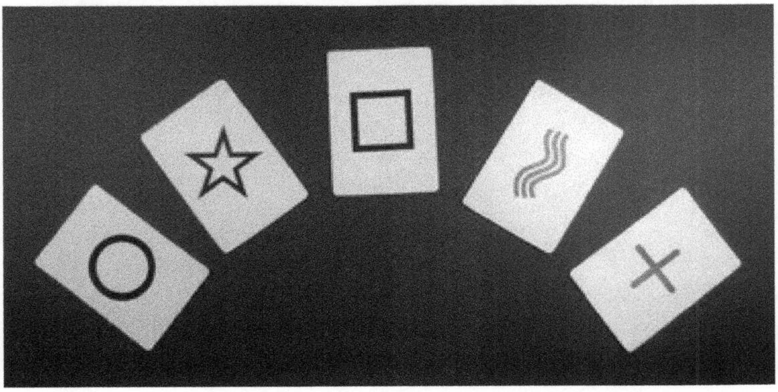

The telepathy experiments at Duke University, which also included clairvoyance and precognition, used specially designed cards called Zener cards. About the size of regular playing cards, these cards were composed of decks of 25 cards, with each card having one of five symbols on one side: a cross, star, wavy lines, circle and square. Using Zener cards under various experimental conditions, subjects would attempt to guess these cards. Out of each deck of 25 cards, 5 correct guesses were expected purely by chance. Using exact binomial probability calculations, it was possible to determine how "improbable" it would be to guess a certain number of cards correctly. In one set of experiments, 2400 total guesses were made and 489 correct guesses were noted. The statistical probability of this outcome is equivalent to odds of 1,000,000 to 1 (against chance) and thus shows significant evidence that "something occurred." Sceptics would argue that factors other than ESP accounted for the deviations (some claimed there was cheating by the subjects, sloppiness by the experimenters, etc.)

Hubert Pearce (left) calling down through a pack of 25 Zener cards (five sets shuffled), before taking a card off.

What conclusions can we draw about Rhine's overall research program? By the year 1940, 33 experiments had accumulated, involving almost a million trials, with protocols which rigorously excluded possible sensory clues (e.g., by introducing distance and barriers between sender and receiver, or by employing precognition protocols (i.e., where the target had not yet been selected at the time subjects made their responses).

Twenty seven (27) of the 33 studies produced statistically significant results - an exceptional record, even today. Furthermore, positive results were not restricted to Rhine's lab. In the five years following Rhine's first publication of his results, 33 independent replication experiments were conducted at different laboratories. Twenty (20) of these (or 61%) were statistically significant (where 5% would be expected by chance alone).

The Rhine Research Centre in Durham still continues to be a thriving centre for Para-psychological research. The good doctor also asked the question 'Do Dreams Come True?' in a 1955 issue of the magazine.

Certainly, Piddington and Braddon were very stimulated by Rhine's article and decided to experiment with telepathy for themselves. At first it was a serious set of experiments to see how much they could correctly get right using thoughts alone. In an interview from 1982, broadcast on 360 Documentaries on ABC, Piddington exclaimed the results would improve the more they tested one another, especially when they applied an effort to concentrate, but in all honesty, it was clearly no real proof that their efforts were based upon anything-more than chance alone.

Major Osmond Dalty, saw a superb opportunity and he suggested that Sydney should devise an act based on the art of telepathy and use it to entertain the other prisoners. This act soon became a notable feature of the prison camp entertainments regime. In fact it became the most controversial demonstration of telepathy ever witnessed, because Sydney, with all of his conjuring skills demonstrated thought transference and telepathy testing in complete silence and used a blindfold to close his visual senses. These two things meant no visual or verbal code could be transmitted. Without the need of sound or sight, Sydney Piddington would transfer randomly acquired information from his mind to the cranium of Russell Braddon. It seemed to be miraculous to-say-the-least.

Changi POW and witness Eric Sutherland Lomax, a British military officer, talks about Braddon and

Piddington in his autobiography ‘The Railway Man.’ (1955).

“Sometimes in the evenings the Australians, Russell Braddon and Sydney Piddington came into the hospital ward to talk. They were experimenting with telepathy and asked for a volunteer to attend their demonstrations. It was eerie, in a darkened prison block, to see them guess the contents of a prisoner’s pockets or the name of a man’s wife, calling up invisible energies as mysterious as radio waves had been to me as a child. We were probably appallingly credulous, but what they did seemed to us real magic in those last months of the war, as the tension mounted towards a barbaric last stand by the Japanese military rulers.”

It seemed that no one quite knew whether to call it a trick or a gift. All Piddington would say is, “you are the judge”.

The day finally came after nearly four long horrific years in the Changi prison camp for liberation to begin; Emperor Tenno Heika of Japan had finally surrendered unconditionally.

Elation blanketed the camp as a billion fears, worries and tears of sadness vanished. Words of thanks were thrown up to God and the realisation that survival had been achieved dawned like a brand new season.

Brave men suddenly became heroes and the final flickers from the fires of war dulled, quietened and fell into fading smoke. The nightmare was over but the dream was just beginning.

Australian Soldiers at the Changi POWs camp Singapore

When Lord Mountbatten arrived in Singapore, he was joined by RAPWI – 'Rehabilitation of Allied Prisoners of War and Internees'. The Americans were the first to leave Changi. Those still remaining were jokingly christened RAPWI 'Retain all Prisoners of War Indefinitely'. When men were repatriated they went to either Sri Lanka or Australia to convalesce. Piddington was released around the 14th of September 1945.

With the experiences of the Second World War behind him, Piddington soon returned to Australia, where he recovered physically, though the war and subsequent imprisonment had installed some characteristics not before present. One of these was the ability to keep secrets; the importance of this would become active in his next endeavours. Another was an accrued talent for manipulating his environment, making things seem one way when really they were another, this was essential when keeping the Changi prison guards unaware of many of the goings-on in the camp, especially the secret radio. Piddington had also returned home having created his own methods in show-biz telepathy. Methods that would remain undiscovered for nearly seven decades and cause many to believe that there was definitely something in the idea that a person could really possess the gift of extrasensory perception (ESP).

At this time in Piddington's life, fate was active in causing his encounter with stage actress Lesley Pope, who would later become Mrs Piddington, and the other half of the most controversial telepathy act the world has ever known.

As mentioned in Braddon's book, Prison comrade Major Ossie Daltry, had once managed a popular West End theatre called the Westminster. In management with him was Miss Kathleen Robinson. Ossie wrote to her by airmail that should she ever need a stage director, he could highly recommend Piddington for his reliability and efficiency.

On the ship back to Australia with Piddington was the actor John Wood, who was one of the Changi actors, he often played the sexy female in many of the early Changi performances. John was given a welcome-home party by the Minerva Theatre Players, of who he was apart before the war. Many were invited, including the cast of the current production. Miss Kathleen Robinson, having just received the recommendation from Ossie Daltry, asked John if he knew Sydney Piddington. He replied with enthusiasm exclaiming he certainly did know him, therefore, Kathleen suggested he was also invited to the party. It was at that party that John Wood introduced the leading actress of the show, Lesley Pope to Piddington. “

Thus begun the new relationship between Sydney and Lesley. They began with much talking which included exchanging stories of life before and during the war years.

They married in 1946, in Woollahra, Sydney, New South Wales, Australia, and the combination of a talented actress and master Manipulatist morphed into 'The Amazing Piddingtons', a telepathy act second to none, baffling to all and credited to one man whose secret methods shook the conjuring world into submission, to this day.

Actually, the creation of the act was also down to the cunning mind of Russell Braddon who developed some of the secret methods Sydney used. He is never credited for his part in the development of the act because this would be admitting the use of trickery, an admission that would have ended the controversy that powered the demonstrations, hence why Braddon refused to discuss the act in great depth in his book.

The newly married couple created a telepathy act based on Sydney's and Braddon's experiments in Changi prison, beginning with a successful show on Australia's 2UE in Sydney and 3K2 in Melbourne, followed by live stage shows.

The Piddington's first radio show was sparked from a conversation with Paul Jacklan, producer and chief at the radio station, 2UE, where Sydney worked, about the Changi camp and the telepathy experiments. Paul thought this could make a good radio show and together they brainstormed ideas of how to turn a visual act into a radio special. They decided to use a trusted panel of judges as the eyes of the audience. It took 3 months to work out a format. Howard Craven, a former radio presenter at 2UE said "*The show took 2UE from the bottom of the heap to sweeping the Australian nation off its feet*". It was also Craven who gave the Piddingtons their first big break in Australia in 1947. The shows would air on Thursday nights and were billed as "*the strangest broadcast ever attempted*" - "The Piddington Show".

The number one show at the time was 'Amateur Hour', but after just 3 Piddington shows, they stole the ratings. 'The Piddington Show' ran for 37 weeks in Sydney, and then aired in Melbourne, then Adelaide and Brisbane. People began experimenting themselves to see if they could be telepathic.

A year earlier on February 24th 1946; the Sunday Telegraph Theatre critic Miss Josephine O'Neil Wrote an article about what she had witnessed in Double Bay in New South Wales;

"These Telepathy tests convinced me. Last Thursday evening, on a veranda in Double Bay, I witnessed messages being passed and received, between two people, without a word being spoken. 27 year old ex POW Sydney Piddington and lovely young actress Lesley Pope conducted their thought transference experiment. Piddington stood by a large blackboard to the left of the veranda, and Lesley to the right, where she could not see the board. Piddington passed onto Lesley the names or descriptions of colours and numbers, even the line out of a book, and Lesley received the message, either by writing it on a slate or by speaking it. As I watched Sydney Piddington demonstrate his powers with Lesley Pope, well, I was convinced!"

By 1949 the couple had saved enough money to take their act to England, staying at the Cumberland Hotel in

Harrow. After a struggle to be noticed by the BBC, they signed an eight weeks contract with BBC national radio.

The shows were separated into 2 series of 4 shows and were a sensational success, so much so, that experts have been trying to uncover their secret methods ever since. In one remarkable program, twenty million listeners waited with bated breath while Lesley Piddington, sequestered in the Tower of London, correctly stated the difficult test sentence from a truly randomly selected book "...be abandoned as the electricians said that they would have no current" relayed by Sydney telepathically from a BBC studio in Piccadilly, several miles away. The text had been chosen independently of the Piddingtons, and it was only revealed to Sydney when he was asked to concentrate upon it in the studio.

Throughout these BBC radio shows, the tests were rigorously controlled, and if there was a code, as so many theorists suggested there was, it would have to have been independent of verbal and visual signals and able to operate at an obstacle infested distance.

The possibility of concealed electronic devices, in a period long before micro transistor techniques and wireless earpieces, was also ruled out by searching the Piddingtons. One by one each ingenious "explanation" of trickery was eliminated under conditions that precluded codes and confederates.

Everyone had a theory about how they might have achieved their effects, and part of the controversy and the success of the shows, was the call to the public, by the Piddingtons, asking them to make their own minds up about whether or not the act was a real demonstration of telepathy or just trickery. At the end of every show they would just say “you are the judge”.

Some paranormal investigators of the subject, including talented Dr. Samuel G. Soal, a British mathematician and psychical researcher, objected to the telepathy shows on the grounds that the Piddingtons were getting the attention that his research deserved more-so, and he insisted that telepathy tests should be restricted to laboratory investigations.

Dr. Soal was partly moved to begin making his first Parapsychological studies following the death of one of his brothers in the First World War. Like many of the bereaved at the time, he made enquiries of mediums concerning communication with the departed; but conducted his observations with a scientific approach. His observations surprised conventional understanding even within psychical research. Most especially, he reported a case of apparently precognitive telepathy of a situation yet to occur for a long-forgotten, but still living, friend of his, Gordon Davis. This suggested, in line with earlier speculations, that the statements of mediums had nothing to do with "spirits of the departed," but only knowledge gained - by telepathy, if need be - from the sitters themselves.

However, the unfathomable Piddingtons made telepathy a topic of conversation throughout Britain, and even years later, there had been no discovery that any part of their act was conceived by deception. Sceptics from all walks of life have never offered a viable explanation, other than it was all a shameful hoax by the BBC that could account for the Piddington's performance, a hoax that the BBC somehow achieved back in the Changi camp and again in Australia in 1947.

So, the journey to stardom was long but fascinating for the Piddingtons. In 1950, following a national tour of the theatres, the BBC offered the Piddingtons a further three broadcasts. These included the amazing and now famous 'Stratocruiser' broadcast, where Lesley received the line from a book while isolated thousands of feet up in a BOAC passenger plane, an event captured on film by British Pathe that can still be viewed today. The act however had a short career. They decided to move back to Australia and start a family. Sydney was offered a job at the Digest magazine heading up the advertising and marketing department. Between 1953 and 1959 they had three children; Mark Sydney John Piddington, Kaye Jennifer Piddington and Anthony James Piddington.

Sadly, the marriage ended and Sydney and Lesley went their separate ways. Years later in the 1970's, Sydney met Robyn Delca Anne Greig and resurrected his famous act for a charity event in Australia, teaching his methods to Robyn who he later married. They toured the show with the same success and still no sign of how it was done emerged. The new Piddingtons had a child, Edwin Sydney Piddington. It is not known if any of the secrets were ever shared with his offspring.

The act soon came to an end, the secrets of its success remaining undiscovered, and on 29 January 1991, in Leura, Blue Mountains, New South Wales, Australia, at the age of 72, Sydney Piddington died after losing his battle with throat cancer. It was believed that his secrets died with him. Lesley Pope later suffered dementia and lost all memory of the Piddington years, it was believed she had also taken the secrets with her. Robyn Greig left show business and ventured into the property industry. It was assumed Piddington's Secrets would never be truly known.

However, as I revealed at the start of this book, this is not true. The Piddington secrets survived both Sydney and Lesley and now for the first time, you can learn exactly how they did it!

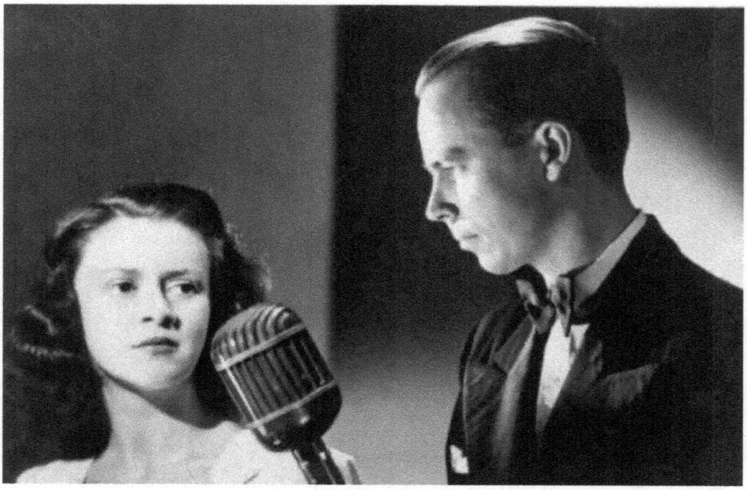

Lesley Pope and Sydney George Piddington 1947

2 THE DISCOVERY

. . .

Sydney Piddington believed that the use of secret assistants, hidden tools of the trade, was perfectly justified. He did not consider this cheating in any way. Gimmicks and tools are used in magic all the time and a 'person' acting undercover was just another tool from the magician's box of tricks. He wanted his accomplices to know it was acceptable to be a secret assistant.

The first thing Sydney realised was that people got nervous if they knew they were doing something considered to be wrong. The heart rate increased and the sweat glands opened up. It can be obvious to an onlooker that a person is acting suspiciously or in fear of discovery. So, he taught a lesson about a special statement that he called "The Honesty Statement".

The Honesty Statement:

The 'honesty statement' is something you may not have associated with magic before because it has been a well-kept secret, mainly due to it being hidden within the opening presentation and not the trick.

The human belief system is complex, but one thing never fails to convince in almost every situation, especially if delivered properly, is the idea of honesty or the 'honesty statement'. The true masters of this are called con-artists, charlatans, 'Scam-artists', confidence-tricksters. It is a strange phenomenon that always seems to work. Let me explain how. When the escape artist says to his audience 'these are real handcuffs', the audience accepts they are real handcuffs, even without third party inspection. This is the power of the 'honesty statement'. Think about it; why would we not believe the handcuffs are real? Surely they must be real in order for the escape to be a challenge for the artiste. Who would ever fake an escape from fake handcuffs when all it will mean is cheating? No one wants to feel they won through cheating, it's not the human way, there is just no satisfaction in it, nothing to be proud of, no true reason to celebrate and surely it leaves a nasty taste in the mouth of the conscience. Yes, the handcuffs are real, how else can he morally enjoy his applause?

Some 'honesty statements' have more impact than others. For example; 'the box is empty' yet a woman appears in a flash. This is a weak honesty statement because we hear something different when it is said. We hear; 'the box *appears* to be empty' and that is our true perception. Our immediate reasoning is that we can see the box is empty but we know there is a hidden compartment somewhere. Nevertheless we still enjoy and wonder at the illusion albeit in wonder of where the secret compartment is. Our minds are just set up to question everything unusual.

So, the 'honesty statement' is a complex statement that can deliver itself in a variety of ways to generate a variety of reactions. Sometimes the 'honesty statement' is visual, such as when we are shown the empty box or the floating table which has no supporting wires by passing a hoop around it, but in many cases this generates a new questioning of logic and immediately our brains seek other ways to understand what we are seeing, for example, the magician tells us there are no secret wires, so we may assume a rod is in in play, somehow.

The point is that the 'honesty statement' can be a very convincing. The impact of the statement is the difference between a tittering applause and a standing ovation, which can also be seen as the difference between an unknown magician and a famous one. The truth behind the 'honesty statement' is that it is a 'dishonesty statement' and it is this dishonesty that very few people see.

Knowing how and when to use the 'honesty statement' is very important. If you use it for every trick it will lose its power and the effect will be weak. However, if you use it as your rule of performance you then infuse it with much power. Let's examine this concept deeper.

Imagine I am a very famous conjurer and my rule of performance is not to be underhand, not to cheat or use confederates in my act. So my 'honesty statement' is that "there are no actors, stooges or camera tricks used in the show". Now you know of this and where my morality is seated, you may watch my show.

When a performer of magic turns an 'honesty statement' into a 'moral statement', the power of the statement intensifies for example, though it is unsaid and just presumed, the 'honesty statement' of a clergyman is that he is a good man who cares about people. In many people's minds, this becomes a moral statement regarding his beliefs about how one treats his fellow human beings, thus, the clergyman is trusted with confessions etc. The notion that the clergyman is not who he appears to be does not enter our heads. What we also fail to acknowledge is the clergyman is also human, with his own failings, just like us. He may feel the same emotions, anger, happiness, sadness etc. just like us. As humans, we react to what we observe and hear. Thus, in magic, it is the same principle.

The 'honesty statement' is never more important than for a magician. Kill the idea that you use actors and stooges immediately, or your magical performance, even without the use of confederates, will lose impact.

The 'Added Possibility' Move

Of course, if you are going to use the 'honesty statement' you must also abide by some simple but very essential psychological rules. If you don't, you will be accused and maybe exposed as someone using confederates. As a mentalist using confederates as a tool in certain tricks, it is important to give your audience a second, albeit a false, reasoning about how you did the trick.

Never forget that you are applauded for your cleverness not your dishonesty. For example, if your effect is so impossible that the only reasonable and logical answer is that a confederate was involved, then you kill the effect and dissolve the impact. You can also lose credibility. So what you *must* do when using a confederate is add in something Piddington called the 'added possibility'. For him it was the idea Telepathy could be real. Let's look at an example of this.

I will summarise a trick that was performed by a famous mind magician and point out the use of the 'added possibility' to you.

A member of the audience is asked to write a word on a piece of paper (a billet) and then fold the paper twice into four quarters to hide the written word from view. The magician points out to his audience while the folded paper is held up for all to see, including himself, that you cannot see through the paper thus it is impossible for him to peak at the word. The magician then reveals what the word is using mind reading. This is a good example of 'added possibility', because now the audience, if they want to, can conclude that when he showed the paper as being opaque, it did in fact allow the magician to see through the paper at the word, somehow, although how is still a mystery. This is important because, in fact, that is *not* how this trick was achieved. Without this 'added possibility' it would be very easy to accuse the magician of using a stooge, although in this case the stooge was his electronic Bluetooth pen that recorded the word for the magician to quickly glance at when the pen was being returned.

The point is that the use of the 'added possibility' hides the true method used, because if the true method was ever discovered or even merely thought of as a possibility, the impact of many other tricks, using the same method, would be destroyed.

Another good example of 'added possibility' is when the magician claims to be using his knowledge of human behaviour, or a skill in influencing others what to pick, say or think. This is done to hide the simpler truth behind achieving the effect, such as simple choice-forces or peak methods.

So Piddington wanted his fellow conspirators to remember this rule when performing the impossible. The last thing a magician wants to do is leave the audience with only one logical conclusion, that you used a stooge, especially if you did.

The use of secret assistants is an art in itself and if used properly can serve the magician very well. So let me take you into the world of undercover actors in magic.

To create the best illusions, you MUST deceive the audience! It is all about achieving the highest impact from the illusion and if this is better achieved using a secret assistant or an 'instant stooge' then of course you should use actors and stooges in the show, and if you want to create a 'miracle' illusion on TV, do use a camera trick or two if it serves your purpose.

There is no *moral* code in magic, everything is a trick and that's why we call these illusions, 'tricks'. You will find that most magicians agree with using confederates in magic although until now, the subject has never been openly discussed or published.

Let's face the facts; fooling an audience is never achieved within the law of morals, a fact Piddington shared with my Grandfather George.

It is acceptable to be dishonest. In magic the audience know you are deliberately fooling them, but nonetheless they thank you for it. In fact, the bigger your dishonesty is, the bigger and better the impact and appreciation.

The use of a confederate does not always have to mean the use of a person. Often an electronic or chemical confederate, designed to feed you secret information, or secretly print a prediction *after* you have been given the information, can be used, these are all necessary tools to help create the effect.

No one outside of your act will ever know your secret and nor should they know. You will tell everybody, every time, that there are no actors, stooges or camera tricks used in the show and most of your audience will believe you because it is an 'honesty statement'! The Piddingtons added a convincer to the mix by offering ten thousand pounds to anyone who could ever prove they used confederates or secret devices in their demonstrations, a powerful ‘convincer’ still used today by telepathy acts across the world.

Now, let's take a look at the pure genius behind this particular magical 'honesty' statement. "There are no actors, stooges or camera tricks used in the show".

Immediately the audience believe this to be true. Why? Simply, because you say so. This statement is the serious part of your routine, the honesty part, the part before the dishonesty is *allowed* to begin, the part where you look them in the eye and audaciously state, with your hands held high, that you are a moral person with a talent. You are humble and convincing, you are likeable, and you are stating your true inner morality as a fellow human being. You are talented so have no need to cheat in that way.

Why should anyone doubt an honest person like you? They almost never do. You are like the nice guy next door who always gets on well with the neighbours and no one ever guesses you are hiding a cunning secret.

The truth is basic at its core, take away the idea that there are confederates at work, and you become a Wizard amongst human kind, a miracle maker, a talking point, let’s go all the way and call you an absolutely cunningly perfect genius.

The facts are that many mind magicians and illusionists DO use actors, stooges and camera tricks in professional shows. They all use technology, electric or acoustic, for the purposes of misdirection, deception and effect. They use confederates sometimes, more than sometimes and all the time, depending on the style of act - and so did Sydney Piddington.

Why Lesley kept silent:

It is not unusual for magicians to reveal their methods to up-coming talent, for example, British icon, magician Paul Daniels decided to release his secrets at the age of 75 in a DVD release titled 'Bravura'. Paul explains in an interview with 'World Magic Shop's Wizard Review' that in his own lifetime he has lost good friends, like Ali Bongo and the incredible Gil Leaney who was a hidden voice in magic, the magical advisor and writer member of Paul's team for 29 television shows. He died taking all of his knowledge with him, knowledge now lost forever. Paul's DVD contribution to the business is invaluable for the next generation of magicians.

Lesley Piddington took an opposite view to revealing secrets, but as she once explained to my grandfather, this was NOT because she was a selfish person who just didn't want to pass the methods on to future magicians, but because to do so would be 'whistle blowing' or 'letting down' the others who were involved in the tricks. These were people that the Piddingtons were grateful to and were also valued friends. These included some BBC production staff who had not told their bosses of their involvement, undiscovered secret assistants such as my grandfather George Hart and his surrounding family. Sydney's best friends, Osmond Daltry, Russell Braddon, who wrote a book that denied any methods of cheating existed - and Lesley herself who gave such convincing performances. For Lesley to reveal any secrets would expose all of these people and would feel like an act of extreme betrayal.

Here is a short transcript from a recorded interview between Lesley and her Grandson Jesse Cox, taken from his award winning radio documentary, ('*Keep them guessing*'), that hints at Lesley's dilemma in disclosing her secrets to any living soul.

Jesse asks: *"A lot of magic secrets, they get passed down to generations and they get re-performed over and over again, and they very much become a part of that family. Now as a performer myself, if I wanted to bring back the tradition, would you feel like you could pass down this magic trick to your grandson to carry it on?"*

Lesley responds: *"Of course, if I had a grandson who wanted to carry it on, I would have enormous difficulty telling him how to. I don't think it would be possible, because there is an awful lot that I wouldn't be able to tell you, it's hard to explain why I wouldn't be able to. It's just that I wouldn't be able to."*

Lesley explains to Jesse that it is hard for her to explain *why* she wouldn't be able to reveal the methods. I believe she is referring to the fact that even to mention it may hurt others involved, and would certainly reveal that there was confederacy in play.

I believe her loyalty issue is further demonstrated by her admission that she went through some years trying to forget the Piddington days, this being out of a misguided loyalty to her new partner Jack. It seems to me that Lesley may have felt that maintaining the connection was somehow being unfaithful to him. Lesley later realised that remembering the Piddington years was actually acceptable and appropriate because Jack was in fact proud of her past success and fame.

Secret Longevity:

So why was it that no one could ever figure out how the Piddingtons achieved the illusion that they possessed real telepathic powers, this ability to send thoughts and ideas from one mind to another, and at any distance - and through any obstacle? Well, here it is the facts behind the Piddington's telepathy act, no theories just facts. What you are about to discover is amazing, more amazing than the effects themselves.

I had no idea of the size of this story until I looked through the evidence, listened to the broadcasts and saw the most clever of creations, this cunning masterpiece actually working, and while the audiences were growing more and more stumped at every twist and turn, I could see everything clearly, all thanks to my Grandfather George and the incredible part he and my Nan Rachel played in this golden chunk of magic from history.

The answer to this massive question is quite short, it was simply because there seemed to be no other way the information, from Sydney to his wife Lesley, could have been transmitted. Here is an article from the time, reported in the Spectator on the 20th of January 1950. (Page 5)

"The Piddingtons' act on Monday must go very far to discomfit their critics. If anything more watertight than

the technique then adopted can be devised I should be very glad to hear of it. Mrs. Piddington was in a diving-bell in twelve feet of water in a tank at Surbiton. Mr. Piddington, with a good many other people, was in a studio at Broadcasting House. Members of the audience were asked to mention numbers at random; the numbers were added together and a book—a volume of Buckle and Monypenny's Life of Disraeli, provided by the B.B.C.—was opened at the page indicated by the total number; somebody chose line 5, and the line was written on the blackboard—" I waited a day after Stanley's ultimatum, and then told. . . ." A moment's pause and then Mrs. Piddington's voice came slowly worrying the thing out—" Waiting . . . all day . . . for Stanley's . . . ultimatum . . . and then." Not word-perfect, but near enough to be astonishing. If not genuine telepathy, what?"

Here was a man in the middle of London transmitting a line from a book to his wife who was under water in Surbiton. Sydney always transmitted his thoughts in hush-silence, thus there was no talking between him and Lesley, so witnesses could *not* conclude a spoken code was in play. The subject matter was randomly selected and all this was being scrutinised by a studio audience made up of up to 300 people, plus a trustworthy handful of authenticated judges and studio persons. All these witnesses plus a listening audience of over 20 million people - and still - no one could identify any method of cheating, misleading strategies or even a glimpse of good-old-fashioned bare faced lying. As far as could be judged, the Piddingtons must have really been telepathic. Even the scientists took an interest in their act.

Test-after-test astounded millions; all kinds of efforts were made by Sydney to further prove-away any theories that people had about how they did it. If you said it was a secret transmitter, the Piddingtons were thoroughly searched beforehand by real police and even dentists to prove they hid no secret devices upon their person, inside their bodies or bags. If you ever suggested Sydney was secretly writing messages to Lesley, using a pen and paper hidden in his trouser pocket, and passing it on using sleight of hand techniques, Sydney would prove it to be wrong live on the air. Witnesses would be called upon to testify against the idea being possible because his hands were never inside his pockets.

Every theory that anyone offered was quickly dismissed. Secretly, Sydney would enjoy the many suggestions people had and he liked the fact no one could figure out his cunning. His friend Russell Braddon would write home to his Mother in Australia and boast about it. In fact, it was good to know what people were thinking because it proved to him that no one was getting close to his methods, and if they did begin to see through a method, he and Braddon could quickly create a new trick and a new method that would disprove that particular idea, thus bringing the theorist back to surface-scratch level. Sydney used their final BBC broadcast to achieve much of this mission. He ended with a repertoire of repeat tests, from the series, and he had adapted them to use more controls to make them more impossible.

Once I became aware of how the Piddington's tricks were implemented, I listened to the broadcasts and watched the television programmes with a different mind-set. There were times when the Piddington's made mistakes which could have led to their secret being discovered. For example; during the final broadcast of the second series, Lesley became flustered in a live-to-air test in the studio. This may not have been obvious to anyone listening, however, as I know what went wrong in the trick and why, I realised her voice sounds concerned on the recording as she obviously fears another error. Or that Sydney is confused with his own system during a test in the Stratocruiser broadcast, because he makes a big mistake that he has to correct and fast. I will tell you all about these events later.

Lesley and Sydney Piddington in Hyde Park London

3 PIDDINGTON'S GRID

. . .

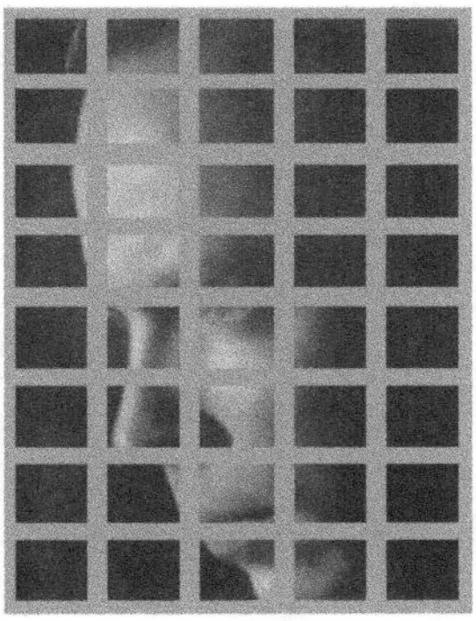

In this, the most revealing chapter, I will mention some of the telepathy effects achieved by the Piddingtons and how they were crafted including the deeper details behind these tricks. The information comes from witnesses who worked behind the scenes with the Piddingtons. These are Dave Daye and his wife Bridie, Rachel Hart and husband George, who made written notes and drawings at the time. Recollections were later shared with Rachel's son Brian Hart senior and his sister Vivian Goldstein.

The Piddingtons used a variety of methods to achieve their mind reading effects, but by far the best and most used by the Piddingtons has been a system kept a secret for six and a half decades. And this is one of the most incredible systems ever invented for the Piddingtons' telepathy act. This is a system, which in my opinion, would still work today and be just as baffling as it was for the millions the Piddington's fooled with it many years ago. This is the system my Grandfather George Hart had to learn. George wrote down Piddington's Grid system in his RAF notebook and used this to study it, learn it and, eventually, deliver it.

Piddington's Grid System

Piddington's Grid was devised by Sydney Piddington inside the Changi POW camp. The grid system was not new in terms of coding and decoding information. The war used a variety of grid style systems as keys to unlock and gather coded information and make deciphering codes easier and faster. For Sydney Piddington, it was a matter of using a grid to organise a secondary system he called 'recall'. A system that could easily operate inside the mind, a visual mind-map completely capable of recalling unlimited information fast. It could also communicate new information slowly.

To understand the 'grid' we must first understand the recall system Sydney used.

Piddington's Recall System:

Sydney Piddington was one of a handful responsible for running a secret radio in the jail. He would secretly listen to about 12 minutes of BBC news late at night and commit all the facts and figures to memory. It was too dangerous to write anything down. The punishment for operating a radio was death by decapitation. To achieve the task of remembering the facts in the news accurately, Sydney used visualisation techniques to help him recall this information the next day.

Sydney explains his recall method in an interview with Cathy Gallon in 1982 on Australian radio station 2UE;

"It was too dangerous to write the news down, so we had to create mental pictures and use visualisation and we discovered by doing this we had tremendous recall and it was a tremendous aid to memory. I went back to my school days where I had studied a simple memory system. Russell and I evolved a plan in Changi to use, what we called visualisation, as a memory aid. So I use to remember ten or twelve minutes of war news, facts and figures and information each night, which I then had to recall in the morning and relay to the officers and men.

It works on a system that we call Keys and Key-words, it involves forming a list of key-words, for instance, if you say 1 to 5, number 1 is represented by an 'L' because it has one stroke, number 2 is represented by 'N' because it has two strokes, and number 3 is represented by 'M' because it's three strokes. Then from those key letters you form key words; 1 becomes Owl, 2 becomes Noah, and 3 becomes Maypole, and when you want to relate what you heard, you say you heard that they attacked France, and there were two thousand men killed on the beaches, you put a picture of an Owl in a boat landing on France and crying because two thousand men had been killed.

And strangely enough as soon as you say number one, you think of Owl, and you see what the Owl is doing, and what the Owl is doing, landing on the beach and crying because two thousand men had been killed floods back into the mind. It's just a recall from what I call a 'key-word' and that can go on up to a hundred or a thousand" (Sydney Piddington).

I will now explain how the Grid system used in the act worked. I will break down the explanation into three parts to clearly show why it was never discovered and how it was capable of operating in complete silence.

Part 1 of 3:

Imagine you are looking at a chess board, except all the squares are white. The board is made up of just 25 squares. Five columns across by five columns down. This is all the space Sydney needed to run his secret grid system and achieve some convincing telepathy effects. Any randomly chosen name, colour, shape or word could be fed to the 'receiver'. To understand the grid clearly I will focus on the letters of the alphabet and how these were used inside the grid to make silent mind reading appear possible.

Placed inside each square is a single letter of the alphabet. The letter 'X' was not used as it was deemed obsolete. I will explain why later. The first square in the top left hand corner represents the letter 'A' and then the letters B, C, D and E ran across the top line. Imagine, the numbers 1,2,3,4 and 5 written above each column and 1,2,3,4 and 5 printed down the left hand side to number the 'across columns'. It was now possible to name any of the letters of the alphabet simply by naming the grid reference numbers. For example, the letter 'S' is situated at grid reference 4 by 4, or 4 down by 4 across.

It is true that during the Piddington shows such a grid was never seen, nor heard, but this was the genius of Piddington's Grid. It was completely silent and to those who knew nothing of its existence, completely invisible because there never was a physical copy of the grid in existence, except for the one my Grandfather drew for himself. This truly was a cunning masterpiece by Sydney Piddington because the grid could only be effective when using his recall system. The keys were the grid reference numbers. If I told you the grid reference 1.1 (1 by 1) (The top left hand corner of the grid), you would remember the letter 'A' is inside that square.

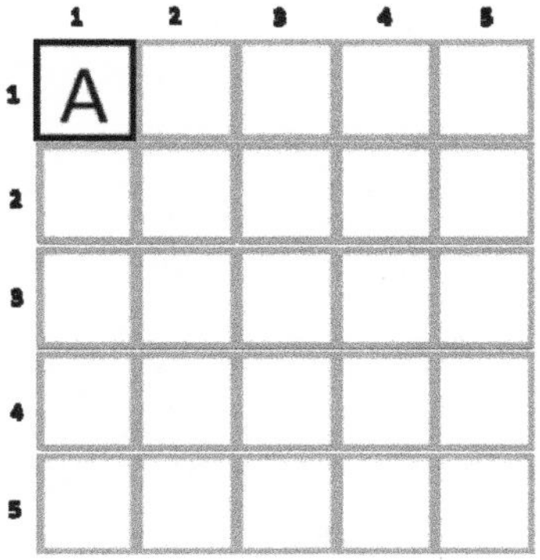

The grid system was a brilliantly conceived. It created the illusion mind reading was the only possible explanation for how information could be received. As I remarked earlier, the letter 'X' was never included on the grid due to the fact no word or name they would use could begin with this letter. It also allowed the grid to work, because the system incorporated the use of a confederate's ten fingers and 26 squares were too many for the fingers to cope with. A person would need 11 fingers otherwise. The grid had to be 25 squares, 5 across by 5 down, thus another reason the 'X' was sacrificed.

Sydney knew that current mind reading acts used a spoken word code, but more importantly he knew that audiences knew of the existence of this code too. Sydney hated the idea of anyone being wise to how the magic was done. When challenged with the task of creating an ESP illusion that did *not* require a spoken code, he turned to Major Daltry and Russell Braddon for inspiration. Together they brainstormed various methods and ideas.

These included using Morse code disguised as general coughing in the audience, but in practise this was too obvious, and most of the camp would be able to identify it. They considered the idea of using stooges but this would result in the repetition of the tricks being almost impossible. However, later on, after the war, Sydney did not dismiss the idea of using stooges completely, if used correctly, these could be used to hide his grid system and pull off some extremely convincing distraction effects.

It was obvious to them that the act would indeed require a secret assistant; they both agreed that neither of them could really read minds. Somehow they needed to find a way of informing the other of what was being written on the blackboard or selected from a list.

The idea for the grid system arose suddenly, without warning. Sydney told my Grandfather that one day he saw a fellow prisoner use his fingers to indicate to another prisoner how many minutes he would be before attending to a request. The message was given in silence. Sydney looked down at his own hands and realised that hands were the most naturally exposed things in the world; he also knew about hand signals, silent signals which were used when communicating various tactical manoeuvres to fellow soldiers, usually when talking would risk alerting the enemy to their presence. Looking at a person's hand for signs of a code was undetectable too, especially if no one knew to look in the first place, and if attention was diverted elsewhere. As a magician Sydney knew much about misdirection.

As the creative process began to roll, Sydney saw one flaw in the grid system, the blindfold! However, it soon became clear that if the secret assistant was positioned in the right place, lower down and over to the left or right of the reader, it would not only be possible to look down the blindfold to see the hands in action, but the blindfold itself would hide the eyes completely, hence no attention would ever be drawn to the secret assistant. It would also kill any idea signals were ever being visually observed.

Now all Sydney needed was a system that limited the movement of the hands to almost zero. There could be no noticeable gesturing. Over the next gruelling two weeks the development of Piddington's Grid was completed. The men rehearsed the best way to make the hands look natural on the lap and how to use the fingers so it wasn't obvious what was going on. I will explain how this was achieved later.

Secrecy was of valuable importance. Only three men knew about the grid, Major Osmond Daltry, Russell Braddon and Sydney himself. At first none of them trusted anyone else with the secret. This was too brilliant to risk blurting around. Although the men could keep secrets from their Japanese captors, it was much harder to maintain confidentiality within the ranks, mainly due to boredom. Most conversational material had sadly dried up between the men, hence the need for some fresh entertainment in the camp. Sydney's mind reading demonstrations were about to be tested as the three men performed to small groups around the stockade.

Sydney Piddington, one of a brave select few risked his own life, to run the secret radio in Changi. He used a memory recall system to help him remember the facts-and-figures he had heard in the news. *(See page 65).* Sydney could recall names, dates, numbers and times simply by creating cues, or 'keys' as he called them, to recall a piece of information.

To remember the many station names on the Central Line Tube in London, he would give each name an identifying set of letters. Tottenham Court Road would simply be 'TO' and Epping would be 'EP'. This was deliberately simple, and that's just how Sydney wanted it to be because there was so much to remember, he didn't want to forget what the keys meant, so each one was easily associated to its meaning.

On his return to Australia, one afternoon on Bondi Beach, Sydney drew the grid in a patch of wet sand and convinced Lesley of its simplicity. He also told her that she could use a simplified version using the numbers one to six, but she needed to learn his recall technique.

Back in the early days of Sydney developing the act with Lesley, she explained that as an actress she was used to learning lines, however, though she agreed with the idea, she felt nervous to use it on the live stage. She had the idea that a mistake would cause embarrassment and ruin the act. At the time this meant Sydney was limited as to what tricks he could create for the act that involved Lesley up front, and this frustrated him. He insisted that Lesley would soon grow use to the grid and would be fine, otherwise it would always have to be Sydney who performed the random choice tricks, where real members of the audiences made real random choices, and if they were to tour around the theatres, more of the content would need to be audience participation led on the live stage. He knew she needed to grasp his grid system fully.

The grid system would become just one of several other methods used by Sydney Piddington in the act.

Knowing that the grid system was more his area of the act than Lesley's, on that beach he quickly knew he had to create some other ways of transmitting information to her. Sydney surpassed himself here, he created some of the most baffling methods the world had ever witnessed and caused many people to believe that their telepathy was real, so-much-so, that the scientists researching such phenomenon would travel to the BBC studios to witness the shows, and the Piddingtons were invited to undertake tests in their laboratories. All invitations of this kind were politely refused. They would surly object to George Hart sitting in the test laboratory and Sydney demanding a platform.

The genius that Sydney Piddington was, managed to create the illusion he could transmit messages and ideas to Lesley at any distance, through any obstacle, at any time, and always, in complete silence. These distance tests did not use Piddington's Grid, instead a different method was used, these telepathy tests were meticulously planned to mix fair play and cunning together.

However, at this stage it may still be difficult to see how this grid made it possible for the Piddingtons to create some of their most baffling studio based mind reading effects. Therefore, let me explain further.

Part 2 of 3: Positioning:

Two things had to happen for the grid system to work;

Firstly, Sydney had to be in front of a microphone that was situated in a position facing his audience.

Secondly, Sydney needed to be able to see the front row of seats from a raised position. He needed to see the people's laps, and one lap in particular, that of a secret assistant, (George Hart). Both of these necessities were easily achieved.

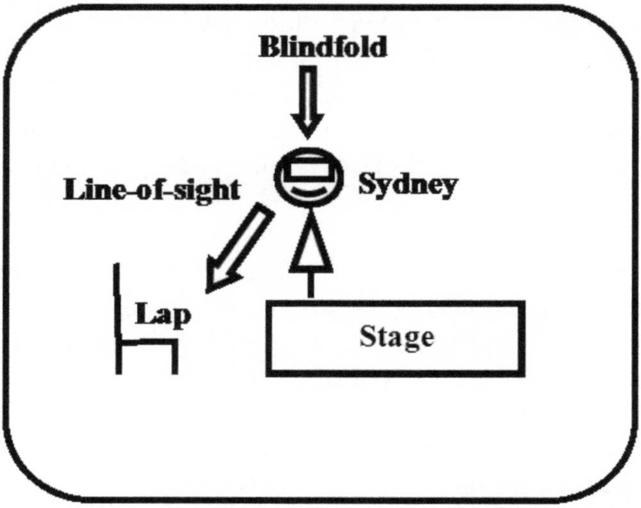

In the 'Stratocruiser' broadcast you can hear Sydney instructing his invited judge, actress Gladys Young, to blindfold him in front of a particular microphone; as he phrases it, "*would you blindfold me in front of this microphone*?" - The one at the front edge of the stage facing his audience and slightly to one side of the platform on which he stood. It just seemed to an audience that he was creating distance between himself and the blackboard, and ensuring that his back was to it. Sydney controlled every detail of his performances, thus it was easy to ensure all went according to *his* plan and that he was in the right place when he needed to be.

The blindfold used was always a white handkerchief. This was positioned across the eyes and tied at the rear, usually using two knots. If you tie a handkerchief across your own eyes you will notice that although you cannot look straight ahead, you can still see downwards through the gaps sited both sides of your nose. It is a very old magician's technique, but still commonly used today. You will clearly see feet and your angle of sight will be enough to see the laps of people sitting in front of you, much more so if you are on a raised platform, as the Piddingtons always were when using the grid system.

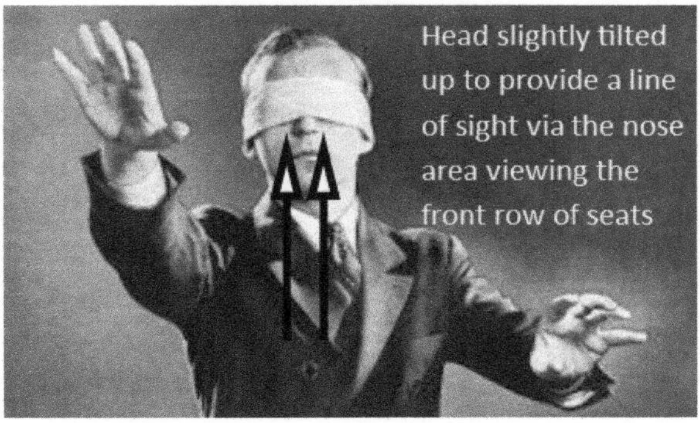

Number 1 Piccadilly Studio

Showing distance from platform & line of sight

It is interesting to imagine what Dr. Rhine would have said about the Piddingtons if he was asked, so allow me to digress for a moment. This is what happened when Rhine was asked about a similar couple of conjurers, although they claimed their sixth sense true whereas the Piddingtons did not. In 1957, Col. Frank F. Carr of the U.S. Army Intelligence Board had written to Professor J. B. Rhine, the head of the parapsychological research laboratory, about a case that was in all the papers at the time: William Foos and his Paroptic daughter, Margaret Foo. Here is the letter:

U. S. ARMY INTELLIGENCE BOARD
Fort Holabird, Baltimore 19, Maryland

AICBD

19 August 1957

Dr. J. B. Rine
Parapsychological Laboratory
Duke University
Durham, North Carolina

Dear Dr. Rine:

A representative of this office recently attended a demonstration of alleged Psychic Phenomena by Mr. William Foos, of Richmond, Virginia, and his associates. During the demonstration it was stated that a similar demonstration had been performed in your presence.

If you did in fact witness the subject demonstration, this office is seriously interested in your evaluation of the demonstration and your reaction to the claims of Mr. Foos.

A reply at your earliest convenience will be appreciated.

Sincerely yours,

FRANK F. CARR
Colonel, U. S. Army
President

Rhine responded by disclosing the blindfold methods used by the couple in this correspondence from August 20th 1957. This is an exact copy of his letter.

Dear Colonel Carr

I have your letter of inquiry about Mr. Wm. Foos of Richmond, Virginia.

Mr. Foos and his daughter did demonstrate in this Laboratory what he represented was the ability of his daughter to read and perceive objects when effectively blindfolded.

The demonstration was, however, a complete failure so far as his claim was concerned. He did not demonstrate any success whatever when provision was taken to exclude the possibility of the girl peeking. He apparently is having is having his 'success' in the demonstrations because of the fact that with the appearance of elaborate blindfolding, most people are deluded into thinking that no trickery is possible. This is, however, an old stunt, as the literature on the subject will show. Yet every generation seems to be a good audience for such a performance, because there are always enough people who do not know what can be done under a blindfold.

If Foos demonstrates for you again, take a heavy towel and put it over her face and under her chin and tie it loosely behind her head. If she objects that it is smothering her, as she probably will, just hold the towel between her and the object she is trying to identify or the paper from which the writing is written.

Of course, there are other tricks to watch out for. It is better to let here identify playing cards than to write something down and better to keep Mr. Foos himself from seeing the cards.

I wonder, of course, what he is up to with you folks. This makes about the tenth or twelfth time I have answered this question. So Mr. Foos at least deserves E for effort, but not, I fear, for some of the other virtues.

Sincerely yours,

J B Rhine

Similarly, the secret assistant, known as the "Grid Operator" or "Exchange," sitting in the front row slightly to the left or right of the reader, would feed letters off the grid system to Sydney or Lesley in complete silence.

The information was given by the secret assistants' right hand resting naturally on the lap. The hand was used to indicate the downward grid reference number. A simple show of fingers is all it took. However, the fingers did not show a number in the way you would expect; this would look far too obvious should someone accidentally look in that direction. The judges were usually seated on the platform facing the audience, thus a visually quiet technique was essential.

Imagine that all your fingers rest separated so none are in contact with the other fingers. There is a 'V' shaped gap or space between each of the fingers. This represents grid reference number 'One'. If fingers were tight together, thus touching, those numbers of fingers were counted to ascertain the number being communicated. This meant that fingers did not need to be bent out of sight or looking suspiciously un-natural. If any two fingers were tight together, then the number being told was 'two'. Three fingers touching signals the number 'three' and so on up to number 'five'. Both hands operate the same rule.

Likewise, the secret assistants' left hand rested on the lap and was used to indicate the 'across' the top grid reference number. Remember the grid is only 5 by 5 squared, so the hands never have to make gestures, they just have to sit naturally on the lap and show the right number of fingers. If done naturally without taught gestures, it is impossible to notice the code is in play. Once learned, practised and applied, Piddington's Grid is a whole new language of communication. It is totally invisible, without any sound and it is adaptable beyond measure. Using this system a person can sit surrounded and seemingly communicate a thought with a second person in the same room, in complete silence. Here is a sample of the 25 finger positions.

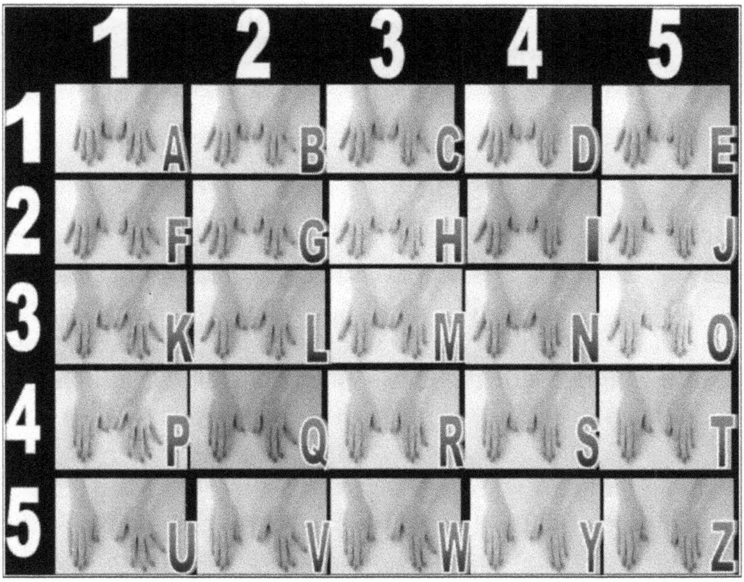

Using the grid meant once a word or name was printed in chalk on the blackboard, the secret assistant could tell Sydney Piddington what the first letter was. Sydney would indicate that he was ready to receive this letter by asking the audience to 'concentrate'; this was a cue word for George to show the relevant grid reference. The cue word also confirmed to George that his hands could be observed and that Sydney was ready to read the grid. Sydney would usually talk again, saying anything to cue the second letter of the name or word. From only these two letters, Sydney knew the answer and the rest was play acting. If the test was to identify a choice from five or six variables, George would indicate a number from one to six using a secondary system that only required George to use one hand. Each number represented a particular choice. It was a matter of memorising which number referred to which choice. This numbers system is called the ‘Abacus’.

Lesley Piddington preferred to use the ‘abacus’ system over the grid reference system, as it was more straight forward. There was less to recall and she could spend more energy on her actual stage performance.

The grid was very powerful for Sydney because it meant, for him, that a test could seem to offer so many choices, that to hit on the correct choice always looked better than chance, especially if he could do it twice in a row. However, this also came with a small risk, the more choices there were the more likely it was for choices to begin with the same two letters of the alphabet.

This happened to Sydney in a test which involved asking one of the judges, Hugh Williams, to choose any tube station on the Central line and write it up on the blackboard, the choice he made was 'Stratford'. The secret assistant George Hart gave Sydney the letters 'S’ and then ‘T’. Sydney had learned the names of all the station stops on that line and would recall them easily when given just the first two letters of the name. In this demonstration, broadcasting live on BBC radio to 20 million listeners, Sydney concluded the choice made by Hugh Williams was 'St Paul's’ and he very confidently announced this on the live show. For some reason the letters 'St' recalled this station to his mind. However, he was wrong. The secret assistant had to re-confirm to a confused Sydney the first letter was indeed 'S' after Sydney openly asked for this second confirmation. You can hear this in the ‘Stratocruiser’ broadcast. The letters were given again while Sydney pretended he was still re-concentrating and he very quickly recalled the only other station it could be, the correct station was 'Stratford'. It was just bad luck that the station freely chosen began with the same two letters as another on the same tube line. However, the mistake only made the effect more believable and the applause was loud.

Sydney and Lesley used his cunning grid system to identify all sorts of names, colours, designs and words, all in complete silence and while blindfolded.

Piddington's Original Grid Format (The Mind Map)

A	B	C	D	E
F	G	H	I	J
K	L	M	N	O
P	Q	R	S	T
U	V	W	Y	Z

Choices were usually made known to the audience while Lesley or Sydney was blindfolded and with their back to the blackboard or placard. All the secret assistant did was reference the correct square on the grid to give the beginning letter of a choice.

The grid reference for the name Bob is simply 1 by 2, 3 by 5 and 1 by 2. The grid reference for the colour Red is simply 4 by 3 because only the letter 'R' is needed. Depending on the theme of the demonstration in play, the grid simply adapts to that theme. Sometimes Sydney used two methods in the same effect. While using a different method to deliver the line from a book, spectators or judges were invited to insert a random word into the line that they could make up. This would be the only word to be delivered to Lesley via the grid, one letter at a time.

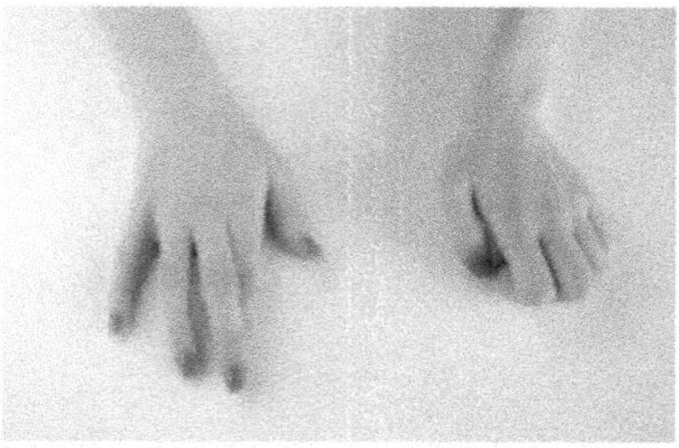

Fingers Crossed = the letter 'X'

If ever the letter 'X' ever needed to be communicated, the Grid operator would boldly cross the fingers as if wishing for good luck. However, the letter was never needed in any of the demonstrations.

Part 3 of 3: A simple trick:

So let me install a scenario here to demonstrate the power of Piddington's Grid. Imagine you have thrown a soft ball into your audience to prove your spectator is truly random, and he or she really is. You ask him or her to write their first name, or even a made up name, on the blackboard behind you. You are blindfolded facing the audience and it is very obvious that you cannot know the name of the person. You have eliminated the possibility a stooge being involved by throwing the soft object into the audience, thus far all has been fair and true. Everything really *is* fair at this point.

Next you ask the audience to concentrate on the name written up on the board. All is silent; no one is talking to you. The audience have been instructed to concentrate on the name. After a period of concentration you speak the name you are receiving in your mind. You are accused of wearing a tiny secret earpiece, or having a Morse code receiver in your tooth and you prove these theories false. You baffle millions, not just once, but every time. No one ever catches you out because you know how to hide it. It is not your only method, merely one of them, and to stop anyone ever discovering your cunning creation, you now do it again, but this time you transmit the name to your wife, who is miles away on top of a mountain.

This is how Piddington operated, just as you were so baffled you were about to look elsewhere to discover him, he would deliberately throw in a "curve ball" just in case anyone suspected he was using a third party, albeit very unlikely, as 65 years of non-disclosure has proved. This allowed him to achieve the same effect using a different method that would dismiss any possibility a third party was somehow feeding the answers to him or Lesley.

A good example of Sydney throwing in a 'curve-ball' can be heard during the final broadcast of the first series, where Lesley is receiving the answers to choices made in a separate studio. In this test no one in the main studio, where Lesley was, could hear anything from the studio where Sydney was, hence choices made were truly impossible to know. However, as Lesley sat blindfolded on the stage facing the 200 strong audience, a printed placard was held up behind her showing only the audience what choice had been made by volunteers in the other studio. This was necessary to allow secret assistant George knowledge of what to inform Lesley. After two successes using the grid, Sydney allows one choice, the final choice in this particular test, to be made in total isolation and in complete silence and without anyone in the main studio ever knowing what the choice was before Lesley spoke it. So, this time there was no placard held up. Lesley Piddington still got it right and this was without the help of secret assistant, George Hart. So how was it possible for Lesley to know what that third undisclosed choice was, unless she could really receive Sydney's thoughts? This is explained in detail in the chapter about the Murder Broadcast *(Page 131).*

The First Confederate Judge:

On the final broadcast of series two, not all the judges were as balanced or just as they seemed to be. Judge Osmond Daltry was cleverly used as a confederate. In the POW camp, Major Osmond Daltry would sit posing as the fair-play Judge and secretly deliver Sydney's grid system while his spectators made their choices. In the camp, Sydney was usually the 'sender' and fellow inmate Russell Braddon the receiver, thus it was Russell who read the grid as Major Daltry sat in his eye-line to deliver it. A sketch, by Ronald Searle of a performance in the camp, shows how they would position themselves. Daltry can be seen sitting lower down and close to a blindfolded Russell Braddon to allow Braddon to covertly see the grid in action on his lap and from the correct angle.

Osmond Daltry **Russell Braddon**

Positioned such, so as to see the blackboard and pretend to be watching Braddon for signs of cheating, he could deliver the grid system undetected.

For good reason, Daltry was invited to be one of the judges on, what was thought to be, the Piddington's last broadcast in the UK. Perhaps, Daltry's history with the development and practise of the methods employed in the act would normally be in direct conflict with his role as a fair-play judge, but as it could be assumed that the public would be unaware he knew any of Piddington's secrets, this was a clever deployment. However, Daltry should not be viewed too harshly here because he was Piddington's master stroke in that particular broadcast and one cunningly designed to further the show.

4 PIDDINGTON'S ABACUS

. . .

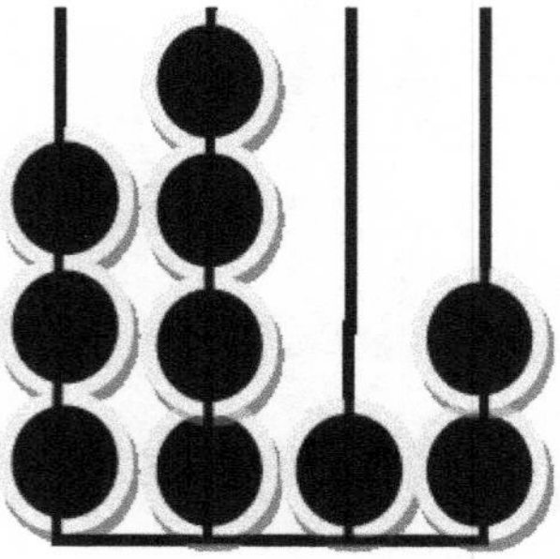

Sydney also invented his secondary system for numbers. He called this his 'abacas' and it worked in a similar way to the grid. A loose hand with all fingers separated was the number '1'. Two fingers touching was the number two and so on up to number '5'. If all fingers were bent creating a loose fist, this was number '6'. All this could be done on one hand and delivered to the Piddingtons one number at a time. The abacas could inform seat positions, rows and longer number sequences.

Using both hands could extend the numbers up to the number '12' and a final position showing both hands touching or fingers interlinked represented the number '13', perfect when using the abacus to reveal playing card values, although this was never used to ID playing cards.

In one test, heard on the final broadcast of 1949, Lesley had to locate a chosen member of the audience; she is caught off guard twice. Once while reading the abacus for a seat location, and again reading it for a chosen number between 1 and 100. The idea was for Lesley to leave the studio while a famous judge chose a member of the audience for her to locate later. On this occasion it was judge, Kingsley Martin who made the choice. On her return into the studio she would always stand on the stage facing the audience, this was so she could read the grid from the correct position. Placing her hand on her forehead as if concentrating was a good way of shading her eyes enough to hide her glance toward the secret assistants' hands.

The abacus would now indicate the row and seat number. The secret assistant would simply use the foot to point left or right, indicating which side of the studio aisle the row was situated.

There were usually only 7 seats in a row in the BBC Piccadilly studios and there were up to 12 rows each side, with a central aisle between them. It was agreed that seat number 'one' began on the centre aisle side.

It is important to mention that the selected row and seat position was verbalised for radio listeners, thus the secret assistant, or ‘grid operator,’ did not need to view the selection by having to look around behind him to see who was chosen. Interestingly there was no code for ‘male’ or ‘female,’ which would have helped in this trick.

In this, the final broadcast, Sydney forgot to verbalise the seat number to the grid operator, although the row and seat was mentioned earlier on by the commentator. This was because Sydney was distracted during the routine meaning Lesley had to guess which of the seven audience members in the row the selected person was. She thought she may be able to notice one of them looking suspicious.

The result was she had to give up and she asked to be told who the person was. She apologised and moved on to the next part in the demonstration.

Next, Lesley was expected to know which number between ‘one’ and ‘one-hundred’ the audience member had picked while she was out of the studio. The choice was the number 'one'. Lesley retook her position on the stage and gave the cue word, “concentrate”, for the secret assistant to reveal the number. Usually this was done in two parts to complete a two digit number, as people usually picked bigger numbers in the belief this would be more likely to fool her. The secret assistant only showed her the number 'one' and because the secret assistant did not move from this number, Lesley felt she needed to cue the second digit with a verbal prod. To do this she acted as if she was receiving only part of the number, she spoke aloud the first number she was receiving, “number one?” she said in an unfinished and questionable tone, but before she could finish saying “concentrate on the second digit of this number” the applause surprised her and she quickly realised everything was fine.

Abacus System

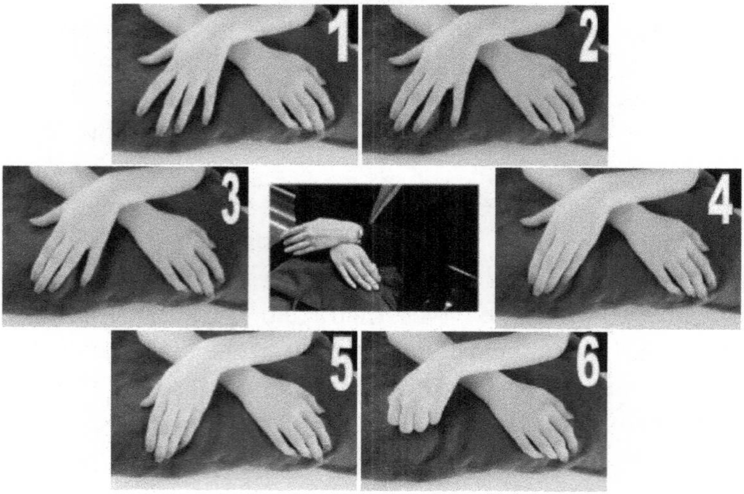

The centre picture (above) demonstrates how the natural seated position looked. As you can see there would be no way of telling that a code was being delivered. Standing up on a stage allowed Lesley a clear view of the front row of seats and of the hands of the confederate, even when blindfolded due to the downward line-of-sight being used when wearing a blindfold.

Tests of telepathy usually involved identifying choices made from a list of five choices, thus the abacus was the perfect tool of communication. If a trick required a two digit number, the Grid operator would deliver each number separately. The same rule is applied should the number be of more than two digits.

In each trick the Piddingtons knew the size of the number they were working with, so it was always easy to read the abacus because they knew what they were looking for.

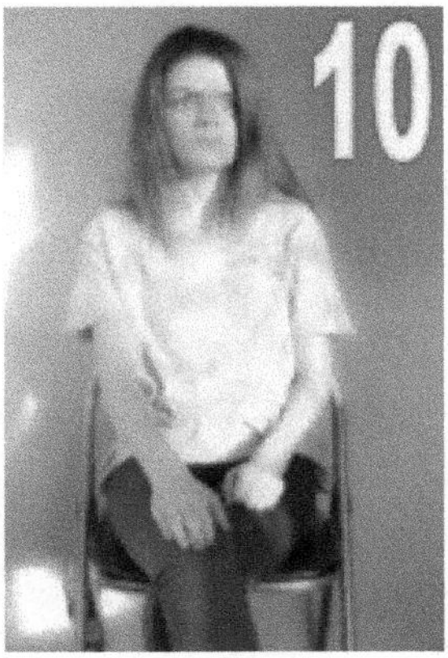

Crossing the legs was a way of informing Lesley which set of choices, or themes were in play. This was used when Kingsley Martin could choose anything from three different sets of choices; Film Stars, Songs or Shapes. If the choice was a film star, then the Grid was used. For a list of Songs, the legs were crossed and the abacus was used. For the list of Shapes, the abacus was used without the legs being crossed, thus Lesley would know which list the Grid operator was coding to her.

The only problem with the early version of the abacus system was communicating the same number twice, a lesson learned by Russell Braddon in the Tower of London broadcast. The first two digits of a longer number, the total of a sum, were 1 and 1 (11…). As he read the first digit as number '1', the Grid operator then moved the hand as a way of closing the abacus and re-opening it up again, so as to deliver the number '1' again. Russell mistook this move as being the next number in the sequence and he saw it as being number '2'.

It was because of this that Sydney decided to introduce a move that would not cause confusion. The move was to be used to indicate the next number was a repeat of the previous one given. Simply by closing the hand by bending the fingers into a fist, but very quickly to avoid mistaking it as the number '6' and then returning the fingers to the number that must be repeated, was a clearer way of avoiding mistakes.

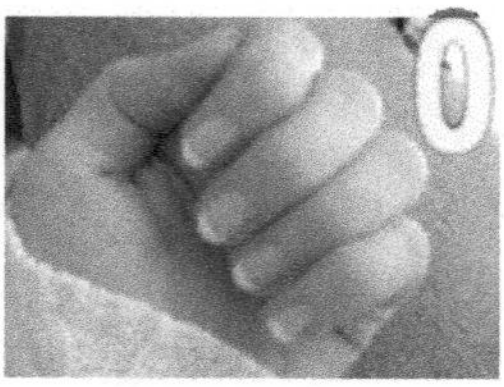

Creating the ZERO on one hand was delivered by a move I call "Zeroing in". The Grid operator would vainly look at their nails by turning the hand over, bending the fingers so as to view the nails and once satisfied they looked great, return the hand to the lap to show the next number.

If the sequence of numbers was finished, the abacus would be shut down by removing the hands from their delivery position. If in the event the sequence needed repeating, the receiver would just ask the audience to concentrate on it ‘more intently.’ In the event a particular number in the sequence needed to be confirmed, the receiver would boldly ask the audience to concentrate on, for example, the third number, or whichever number needed to be confirmed. Often was the case when speaking to the audience, the Piddingtons were actually speaking directly to the confederate.

5 THE STRATOCRUISER BROADCAST

. . .

The 11th Broadcast 1950

Boarding a BOAC Stratocrusier.

In this broadcast the Piddingtons performed 3 amazing telepathy acts; the identification of two randomly chosen London Underground stations and a personal possessions test where random objects were collected from the audience and transmitted over long distance in silence.

The act was seen as a spectacular piece of telepathy for many reasons. The first was that Sydney was, as usual, blindfolded in a London studio. The second was that Sydney was still able to transmit thoughts to his wife Lesley, who was hundreds of miles away out of radio contact flying above Bristol in a BOAC Stratocruiser.

She was accompanied and surrounded by journalists and at no time could she hear anything that was going on in the Piccadilly studios in London. Five judges were closely watching and taking part in the show, together with more than 150 members of the public as the studio audience. 20 million sharpened ears were also listening to everything being said.

The invited judges on this broadcast were dominantly a mix of famous artistes.

Hugh Williams was born as Hugh Anthony Glanmor Williams, and his nickname was "Tam". He was a popular film and stage actor, who became a major film star in the British cinema of the 1930s. In 1930 he toured America in the cast of the R.C. Sheriff play Journey's End and appeared in his first film 'Charley's Aunt' during a spell in Hollywood. He then returned to Britain and became a mainstay of the British film industry. He made 57 film appearances as an actor between 1930 and 1967.

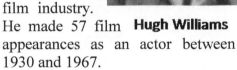

Hugh Williams

Derrick De Marney

Close friend of BBC commentator Stephen Grenfell and guest judge Derrick De Marney was the son of Violet Eileen Concanen and Arthur De Marney, and the grandson of noted Victorian lithographer Alfred Concanen; he appeared on the London stage from 1922 and starred in films from 1928. He is perhaps best known for his starring role as Robert Tisdall, wrongly accused of murder in Alfred Hitchcock's Young and Innocent (1937). Other early film roles include Benjamin Disraeli (a role he also played on stage in Young Mr. Disraeli) in Victoria the Great (1937), and its sequel, Sixty Glorious Years (1938).

Gladys Young was born in 1887. She was an actress, known for The Lady with a Lamp (1951), Kathy's Love Affair (1947) and One Wish Too Many (1956). She was married to Algernon West. She died on August 18, 1975 in Eastbourne, Essex, in England. Commentator Stephen Grenfell introduced her as 'the lady of the silver microphone.'

Gladys Young

Dudley Perkins

The final judge was Dudley Perkins, a lawyer. Dudley was said to have uncovered many fraudulent activities in the recent past and was invited to cast his eagle eye over the proceedings. He spoke with a calm and quite unimpressed demeanour, almost confident he would catch a glimpse of any suspicious horse-play. More about Dudley later.

At the microphone is commentator Steven Grenfell

Stephen Grenfell:

The commentator was Stephen Grenfell who was also an actor and writer, known for The Heritage (1967), Wolhaarstories (1983) and BBC Television Children's Newsreels (1950).

After explaining to the listeners that Lesley was up in the air in a Stratocruiser, thanks to Charles Able of BOAC, Sydney began the first telepathy test. He was blindfolded by Gladys Young at the microphone overlooking Grid operator George Hart in the front row. Sydney had to bend down for Gladys to reach him because he was six foot one.

The stage was set for what was going to become the most convincing test of telepathy ever performed. Sydney had worked hard on this one and Lesley was out of contact with him. She was 150 miles away, 15000 feet up in the air, flying over Bristol. A short wave radio was set-up and used to broadcast from the aircraft to the studio in London, and thus to the airwaves. Lesley was not allowed to wear any headset or have any knowledge of what was happening in the studio.

Nervous, Sydney explains that he has not heard from Lesley all day as she left early that morning and he would like to hear from her. I am sure he must have forgotten that he was telepathic and able to communicate with her via his thoughts at any time. No one ever criticised his comments during or after the broadcast.

Test 1: Name Any Tube Station:

Sydney asked Hugh Williams to imagine he was taking a tube train somewhere and he was using the Central line. Hugh could choose any station from which to board the train and he was to write that name up on the blackboard. To dismiss the idea Sydney was listening to the chalk strokes or counting the letters, Hugh was told to add as many dummy letters to it as he liked. Hugh was also instructed not to write anything until after Sydney was blindfolded.

Once he was blindfolded he had to use the downward glance technique to see George's lap, where his hands were rested. *(See Piddington's Grid).* At first Sydney could not see because Gladys Young had tightened the handkerchief too tight, she added three knots. Sydney used his eye brow mussels to adjust the blindfold but it did not give him enough vision through the gaps either side of his nose. Sydney had no choice but to quickly raise his hand and physically adjust the blindfold. To onlookers this looked like he was just getting more comfortable, but Sydney knew this also looked bad and he needed to reboot the illusion he was blind. He thought fast and asked the Commentator if he was by the microphone, thus giving the false impression he was just worried about falling off the stage.

Stephen Grenfell assured Sydney that he was in front of the microphone. Sydney had got away with fixing the blindfold to allow vision down through the nose area. He could see George's lap position but by this time he was feeling flustered rather than relieved.

Hugh Williams had finished writing the station name 'Stratford' on the blackboard. The commentator informed him the task was complete. Sydney spoke the cue word '*concentrate*' and George showed Sydney grid reference 4 by 4, the first letter 'S'. Sydney cued the second letter simply by speaking again and George gave him grid reference 4 by 5, the letter 'T'. Sydney could now recall the station beginning with the letters 'St...'

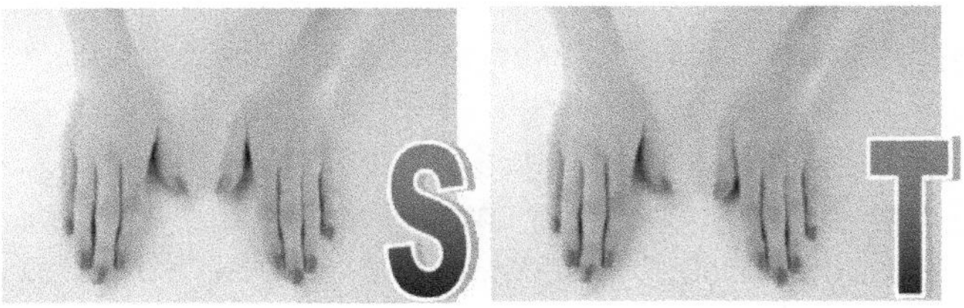

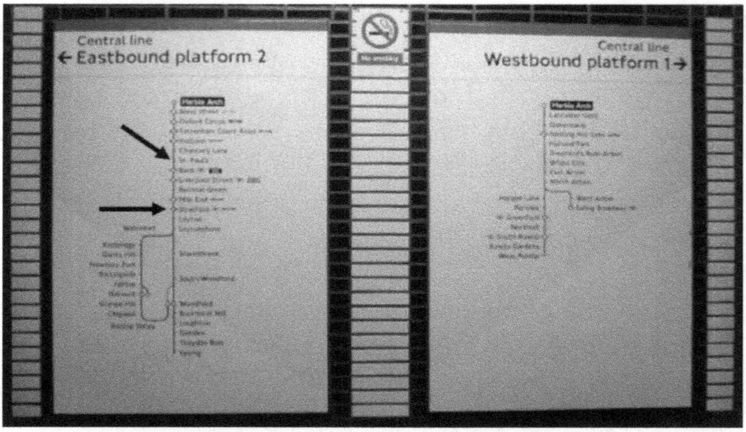

Central Line Stations. Arrows show two stations beginning with the same letters.

Prior to the effect, Sydney had studied the station names on the London Central Line, and was confident he could easily recall any of them once given the right key letters. However, he recalled the wrong station. He blurted out the name 'St Paul's'. He waited for applause but it never came. Confused, Sydney asked if he had got it right and was told by Stephen Grenfell he was wrong. Things didn't seem to be going well at all thus far, but Sydney was not beaten yet. He asked the audience to concentrate again, thus cueing George to give him the key again. Sydney openly asks for the first letter and George shows him the 'S'. Suddenly Sydney realises his mistake and that the station should have actually been 'Stratford'. He confidently blurts this out and the applause is enjoyed. Nerves cause his stutter to play him up, but he continues with the second part of the trick.

Next he asks Derrick De Marney to write up the name of the station he wishes to get off the tube, again on the

Central line. De Marney adds a lot of dummy letters to the name 'Tottenham Court Road' and even underlines his choice. George gave Sydney the grid reference 4 by 5, the letter 'T' and 3 by 5, the letter 'O'. The key letters 'To...' were enough for Sydney to recall 'Tottenham Court Road'. De Marney was slow to finish and Sydney was eager to move on. Sydney asks Stephen Grenfell if he had finished yet, trying to hurry him along. Once he had finished Sydney played his game of concentration and revealed it was 'Tottenham Court Road' quite quickly. He took his applause and began to prepare the first test for Lesley up in the Stratocruiser.

This next test did not use Piddington's Grid, so George could now relax and enjoy the rest of the show.

Test 2: The Possessions Test:

A large envelope was taken into the audience and random people were asked to put personal possessions inside it, something that they would easily recognise again so it could be returned after the test. Sydney also requested that not too many things were collected because there wasn't too much time. The truth here was that Sydney knew how long it would take Lesley to play her part in this test. It had been rehearsed many times. The broadcast was already running behind schedule because of the time it took to complete the first test. The BBC would not hesitate to cut the show off the air if it over-ran.

Once the large envelope had a mixed selection of personal possessions inside it, it was brought back to Sydney who tipped out the contents onto a table.

The Most Secret Assistant:

It is at this point I need to inform you about someone else who was active in the act on this broadcast. His role was to take custody of the large envelope and be the person to collect items from audience members. His name was Ian Messiter and he was the BBC Production manager of the Piddington broadcasts. He was also a very good friend of the Piddingtons, he shared an interest in magic and he knew how every test the Piddington's performed was done. In fact without him, it would have been difficult to have the secret assistants in the audience. Ian Messiter, in a later interview on radio, admitted to the world that he knew everything about the Piddington's methods and vowed never to reveal what he knew, and to his credit he kept his word.

Ian Messiter

In the personal possessions test, Ian Messiter took the envelope into the audience to collect personal items from a variety of people. However, the key person he went to was my Uncle David Daye, who was sat aisle-side near the back. David inserted a small handful of small items that were tucked behind a World War II ration card. The actual ration card belonged to David's wife Bridie Daye. These items were a short pencil, a bus ticket, a ring, a pound note and paper clip. It looked to any onlookers that he had just inserted the ration card. These items were the very ones Sydney would choose to transmit to Lesley ignoring any items inserted legitimately by all the other audience members. The order of items for transmission had already been arranged.

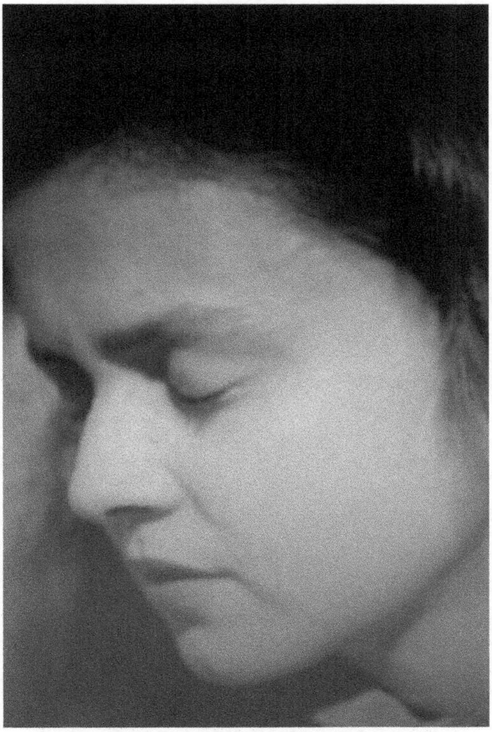

Lesley Piddington concentrating on Sydney's thoughts on board the BOAC Stratocruiser flying over Bristol

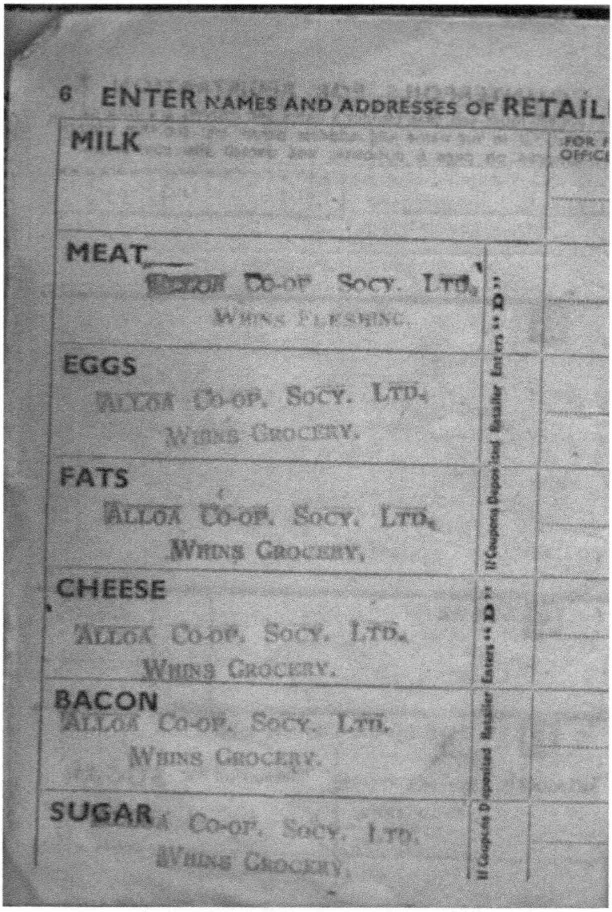

6 ENTER NAMES AND ADDRESSES OF RETAIL

MILK

MEAT
Co-op. Socy. Ltd.,
Whins Fleshing.

EGGS
Alloa Co-op. Socy. Ltd.
Whins Grocery.

FATS
Alloa Co-op. Socy. Ltd.
Whins Grocery.

CHEESE
Alloa Co-op. Socy. Ltd.
Whins Grocery.

BACON
Alloa Co-op. Socy. Ltd.
Whins Grocery.

SUGAR
Alloa Co-op. Socy. Ltd.
Whins Grocery.

If Coupons Deposited Retailer Enters "D"

Sample Ration Card

Ian Messiter returned to Sydney with the envelope and he tipped up the envelope quickly, this was to avoid any of the judges or Grenfell noticing the secret items were inside the ration card. It was a move that had been rehearsed many times before. Sydney pauses to ensure the items he needed were on the table and nothing was still stuck inside the envelope. You can hear his searching pause in the broadcast. All was well, the curse of the show seemed to have lifted and things began to go right.

Lesley Piddington had already studied the items and had learned her lines well. The only problem was Lesley needed to know when to begin talking. They had arranged a clever cue. Sydney would simply inform the second commentator, Gilbert Harding, who was on board the aircraft, to tell Lesley to 'standby'. Once Lesley heard these words she would wait about ten seconds and then begin receiving thoughts from Sydney in the studio.

The secretly added items were undetected as being deliberate additions and it simply appeared that Lesley was actually picking up on impressions of randomly gathered personal possessions.

The idea that there was any kind of electronic device in play was dismissed. Lesley had been searched by female flight attendant, Jean Gordon, after she boarded the aircraft. She talks about her detailed search of Mrs Piddington on the broadcast.

Lesley began to deliver her lines. As an actress it was easy to add drama to her performance. She would always begin with identifying the impression of the item. Sydney always told the audience that he would send impressions of the items not exact details. Certainly on this occasion, it sounded as if she was concentrating hard and actually receiving images of the objects in her mind. Next she would appear to see it clearer and thus able to describe more details about it. Lesley deliberately identified a fountain pen, when it was in fact a pencil and a brooch when it was a wedding ring. It was important to get something wrong albeit the 'impressions' correct, because

98 percent accuracy was convincing while 100 percent accuracy, was suspicious.

When Lesley identified a one pound note, adding that it was a green one, she went onto ask Sydney to think of the serial number that it bared and she began to tell what the serial number was. Of course she was quite accurate as she recalled the number C71B265454 as if she was holding it in her own hand. The bus ticket was identified along with its accurate value (3 half pennies).

Sample Green One Pound Note 1949

The performance was beautifully delivered, but it seemed there wasn't enough time to complete it. Sydney cut her short just as she was going to describe the next item after the bank note. The idea here was to show that the telepathic connection between both minds had been lost simultaneously. They had already shown that Lesley could start a connection in sync with Sydney, so it was important to show they could lose a connection in sync too. The idea was for Sydney to interrupt after the test's finale, the transmission of the serial number from the seemingly random pound note, and say "that is all we've got time for" on that test, thus seemingly disconnecting his thought transference to Lesley. This was the key for Lesley to say, "Start concentrating on the next item", a second time, thus giving the impression that she had also experienced a loss of connection. This was a master-stroke and a pre-planned one, but it failed to hit its target as unfortunately, the BBC engineers faded her mic out a second too soon and her statement never made it to air, although it *is* possible to hear the attempt momentarily.

The faders went up in the Piccadilly studio. Sydney was ready to confirm Lesley's statements had been correct. He asked Derrick De Marney to confirm the articles were all correct. Sydney expected him to remember the fountain pen was wrong and also a piece of jewellery was a wedding ring and not a brooch. De Marney said nothing of this so Sydney reminded him of it on the air.

Test 3: 150 Envelopes:

It was time for their big finale, the demonstration to end their time on the BBC and leave a mark in history.

On their arrival, the audience, made up of 150 members of the public were each handed an envelope containing a blank piece of paper they could write or draw on. Each envelope was consecutively numbered from 1 to 150. The audience was asked to insert anything they liked into their envelope, such as a drawing or a piece of writing.

Next, Sydney asked Judge Dudley Perkins, a lawyer, to freely select any two numbered envelopes. He picked 34 and 88. Sydney then transmitted the contents of both envelopes to Lesley who was flying over Bristol in a

BOAC Stratocruiser. He did this without talking. At no time could Lesley hear anything from the studio. She had been thoroughly searched for concealed devices and as she sat guarded by many Journalists she was able to accurately describe the contents of both envelopes.

Many have theorised about how this trick was achieved, but to my surprise no one has ever described the mechanics of it. Many believe the envelopes were switched or that there was a code somehow hidden in the silence. A few have suggested that Lesley went to her place already armed with the information and that is obviously true, but how did Sydney work this wonder?

The Method:

In the beginning, when inviting the audience to insert or draw something and place it inside the numbered envelope provided, it was important for Sydney to make clear to the audience that writing something on the piece of paper was one of the options they could choose, because he would later receive a piece of paper with two lines from a poem written on it. Despite this, the audience did not receive a pen or pencil to write with, but this wasn't important.

To understand what actually took place we must revisit guest judge and lawyer Dudley Perkins.

More about Dudley Perkins

Dudley Perkins, who was introduced as a lawyer, was in fact a university student and friend of Russell Braddon who had been studying law at university. This was a degree Braddon found to be too heavy-going and chose not to finish it. The Dudley Perkins character was invented for the show. He was the only non-celebrity judge ever to appear in the entire series. He was in fact a stooge and not a real lawyer at all. Here was a student out for a bit of fun and to help out an old chum. He would also fool the world for years to come.

Stooge Judge:
Dudley Perkins selects envelopes 34 and 88

Before this broadcast went to air, the BBC commentator Stephen Grenfell was requested, by Dudley, not to say too much about him in his regular introduction but instead just to keep it brief and move on.

However, unaware of Dudley Perkins being a stooge, Grenfell asked Dudley to say something about himself. This was unexpected so Dudley just confirmed he was there to cast a legal eye over the proceedings. However, Sydney became worried that his number one key stooge may have caused suspicion; after-all, there was no legal issue here. His nerves caused his stutter to act up, which can be heard clearly during the broadcast. Dudley was introduced second, and this was deliberate to allow the real celebrities to distracted attention away from Dudley.

This was indeed a brilliant piece of time-misdirection by Sydney.

Dudley's only job was to pick two numbered envelopes from a choice of 150 envelopes. He simply had to call out numbers 34 and 88. His job was then done.

The two secret assistants, David Daye and Rachel Hart, who sat in the audience held envelopes 34 and 88. They already had these envelopes when they entered the studio. Nonetheless, they were each presented with an envelope along with the rest of the audience when they arrived, but these would be ditched away. The numbers 34 and 88 never appeared on any other envelope.

It was time for stooge judge and fake lawyer Dudley Perkins, to step up and deliver his part in the act. Sydney asked Dudley to choose any two of the 150 envelopes held by the audience. As planned he chose numbers 34 and 88, held by secret assistants Rachel Hart and her brother David Daye. They were both seated nearer the back of the studio in separate areas.

Due to the British Pathe news cameras filming the show, a superb piece of footage is captured of my Nan Rachel Hart handing her envelope to Hugh Williams. She has attempted to disguise herself with a hat and glasses, although the glasses are legitimately worn.

A man who is seen sitting in front of her, is a friend of the family, a neighbour called Joe whose surname is forgotten to us. Knowing what was truly happening he was worried Rachel may be recognised as being part of the audience before as all eyes looked on. Joe looks away as Williams approaches and he holds his breath until the deed is done. His 'cringe' is captured on the film footage.

Secret Assistant Rachel Hart passes envelope 88 to an unsuspecting Hugh Williams. She deliberately wears a hat and glasses

Once Dudley Perkins had called out the two pre-arranged numbers, Hugh Williams was instructed to collect the two envelopes and return them to the stage. It was important for a known and trusted judge to collect the envelopes as this added the credibility Sydney strived for in his methods. Sydney instructed Hugh Williams to hand one of the envelopes to Gladys Young and to hold the other himself, thus Sydney never touched the envelopes and both envelopes were in publicly trusted hands. Stooge Dudley Perkins was slowly being forgotten as the demonstration pushed forward.

Next, Sydney instructed both judges to tear open the envelopes, being careful not to allow anyone to see what the enclosures were.

To Miss Young, Sydney said; "before you show me your enclosure, would you mind answering some questions?" Miss Young agrees.

"Have I at any time handled the envelopes issued tonight?" Gladys Young replies with "No".

Sydney then asked, "Could I have seen the contents in any detail?" with Gladys answering "No"

"Have I touched any of the envelopes since I asked for messages or some other enclosure to be inserted?" Gladys answered with yet another "No".

"Then in your opinion, could I or Lesley have any idea of the nature of those enclosures that you hold and which were determined by numbers announced by Mr Perkins?" Gladys Young replied, unknowingly setting the scene and tension for the audience both in the studio and at home, "No, not possible".

Lesley Piddington ready to receive thoughts about the enclosures from two randomly selected envelopes

At this point Sydney is interjected by Stephen Grenfell, who points out Lesley Piddington's position, that she is isolated in an aircraft thousands of feet up in the air and she has been there for hours.

Contact is once again made with Gilbert Harding in the Stratocruiser who states that the conditions on board the aircraft remain exactly the same. Lesley is still isolated from hearing anything going on in the studio.

Sydney invites Gladys Young and Hugh Williams over to his microphone to show him the enclosures from the envelopes for the first time. Notice that both enclosures are shown at once. This is because it has been pre-arranged that the poem be used first and Sydney could not rely on being handed this particular envelope first, thus asked for both at once.

He also asks the audience, those who can see what the enclosures are to assist him in transmitting them to Lesley.

The audience was always made to feel that their help was needed too. The idea was, the more minds that were transmitting the information meant that the messages would be stronger and clearer and more powerful. This concept also enforced the idea that 'normal' people were truly capable of being telepathic, that it wasn't just the Piddingtons who could do this sort of thing, everybody could channel their thoughts into a transmission!

The other part of the illusion was created by the manner in which Sydney asked for help from his audience. He would be very serious, sound sincere with it and act as if his request was quite reasonable. No one ever suggested that to ask mere mortals to lend their telepathic powers was a ridiculous thing to do. No one ever pointed out that such powers were non-existent in the 'normal' man. It seemed that such a request was rather common under the circumstances and people gladly helped out.

Sydney Piddington at the microphone with Gladys Young transmitting a poem to Lesley

Again Lesley is given the ten second cue as she is told to "Standby". As rehearsed Lesley begins receiving her first impressions of the enclosures through a transmission from Sydney. The hand written poem is the first. Lesley pretends to have difficulty understanding the thoughts. She sees the words 'Spirit' and 'Bird' and then after some figuring out announces she can guess what it is by the impression she has received. It is a poem of two lines;

"Hail to the blithe spirit, bird thy never wert".

Lesley Piddington on board the BOAC Stratocruiser over Bristol smiling after receiving the poem transmission from Sydney's thoughts 106 miles away in London

Lesley is clever to act as if she is excited and surprised by the poem, pleased to hear such beautiful words and glee at such a great choice by whomever inserted it in the envelope. Such a reaction breathes realism into the idea that this is the first time Lesley has been reminded of the selection and concurrently the mark of a talented actress.

Gladys Young is asked to read out what the person has written on their enclosure and it is confirmed as being the same. The applause is loud and Sydney is pleased all is going well. His stutter has softened and he feels safer.

Before Sydney transmits the second envelope enclosure to Lesley, the instruction to 'standby' is given again allowing the Piddingtons to work in sync. Lesley waits ten seconds and begins to receive the image of a started crossword. She dismisses the idea it is a draughts board and lands on the fact it is a "crossword puzzle". Using the 98 percent accuracy rule, they have inserted one word that makes no sense. According to my Grandfather, the truth was that while partly completing the crossword they messed up but decided to leave it in. They were trying to create a correctly incomplete crossword but some of the clues had stumped them. However, this would only show that if Sydney didn't understand what he was looking at, Lesley couldn't understand it either. These small intricate details were all Sydney's ideas.

Lesley identified the enclosure was a crossword puzzle and even mentioned it was only half filled in. She began to see the words after asking Sydney to concentrate on them. They were 'Shuffle' 'Cut' 'Curtains' 'Job' 'Head' 'Audit' 'Dryer' 'Caitiff' and 'Cull'.

Hugh Williams was asked to confirm the words on the puzzle were the ones Lesley had said. Sydney prompted him to mention the errors too. Hugh Williams pointed out they were all correct, but the word 'Head' was in fact 'Cranium' and the word she could not get was hard to understand as it did not spell out a word. It was 'CAITIFF'. Again the Piddingtons had reached their target of 98 percent accuracy. The audience applauded and millions would remain baffled for over 65 years.

Gilbert Harding, on board the Stratocruiser reaffirmed that Lesley could not have cheated as she was isolated. He asked if she wished to say anything and she said;

"Thank you very much everybody and you are the judge".

Gilbert ended his broadcast by confessing that he was baffled. Sydney announced that he always agreed with his wife and the broadcast ended.

Today you can research all the judges from this broadcast and peek into what became of them all, except that of Dudley Perkins, who unsurprisingly has vanished off the face of the Earth never to be heard of again.

Dudley remained unchallenged and totally unsuspected of anything untoward, a true testament to the strategic planning and brilliant use of time misdirection Sydney delivered. And the convincing performance from Sydney Piddington himself.

No-one realised that the Piddingtons had ever used such an out-dated tactic as a stooge, and as they were offering ten thousand pounds to anyone who could prove such persons were ever involved, it was easily dismissed.

5 THE DIVING BELL BROADCAST

. . .

1st show of series 2

Reported on Monday January 30th 1950 in the Townsville Daily Bulletin page 5

"A further remarkable demonstration of their powers was given by Mr. and Mrs. Piddington, the Australian couple, whose 'telepathy act has aroused the Interest of the whole of Britain. For the start which was broadcast by the B.B.C. — Mrs. Piddington was sub-merged in a diving bell. In a tank of water II feet deep. Mr. Piddington remained In the B.B.C. studios at least 12 miles away. A line chosen from a book by members of the audience at the B.B.C. and read to Mr. Piddington. Within a few minutes it was recorded— almost word perfect— by Mrs, Piddington still submerged in the diving bell. During the test she

was accompanied by a famous diver who vouched that she had no apparent communication with anyone during that period. Photo shows Mrs. Lesley Piddington inside the diving bell, ready to be submerged into the tank".

The information in this chapter refers to Sydney Piddington's methods and comes from witness and behind-the-scenes helper, Dave Daye. He shared his account of events with his nephew, Brian Hart during the 1960s and also with his wife Bridie Daye, his sister Rachel Hart, and later, her grandchildren, myself, and my brother 'little' Brian Hart in the 1980's.

Responding to a critical letter he received from a sceptic listener, Sydney reads the critic's closing suggestion to the nation; "If we could really transmit thoughts - why didn't we put Lesley into a trunk, lower it into a pond and try to receive from there?" thus a new telepathic act was born.

In this come-back broadcast the Piddingtons decided that an underwater demonstration of thought transference would bring variety to the show and further quiet many of the theories the critics could throw at them. Theories that frustrated Sydney a lot.

Lesley had always spoken of the dangers of housing the broadcasts completely inside a studio, that to do so would be monotonous and boring to listen to. Plus it led to easy criticism regarding how the act may have worked. However, taking the listener outside, while at the same time creating some interesting obstacles through which to send thoughts, would be a fascinating experience and add an air of impossibility to the performances. Ian Messiter contacted the diving school and test centre in Surbiton to investigate the possibility of an underwater submarine, but was told 'no'. Furthermore such an endeavour would be far beyond the budget dedicated to the series. A diving bell was recommended and that was good enough for Ian.

Siebe Gorman & Company Ltd was a British company who developed diving equipment and breathing equipment and worked on commercial diving and marine salvage projects. They tested a variety of products at a testing tank in Surbiton.

However, Lesley didn't like the idea of venturing under the waves in any contraption. Although Lesley loved the water, spending many wet and wonderful times splashing about on Bondi Beach, being under it was a worrying alternative to her. The idea that it was a testing and development centre suggested a higher chance of something going wrong. She eventually succumbed to the charms of her husband and agreed. She also decided that as she had vented the idea of making the programme more exciting for the listener, she had to agree to this venture.

The 'Tank Room' was a well-lit environment housing a large tall circular drum style tank. It held a mighty 12 feet of clear water in a space the width of an Olympic swimming pool. On this day it was overhung by a six and a half hundred weight steel diving bell suspended on a pulley-cable. Running up the inside of the tank was a blue metal ladder that allowed divers to climb down to the bottom. There were rows of square windows cut into the bottom of the tank, allowing viewing from outside.

The diving bell itself was a dark bell shaped hollow ventricle large enough for two. Inside were moulded seats facing one-another and a steel door that framed a small but thick window. Air was pumped in from outside via flexible pipes and a steady pressure maintained inside.

In this demonstration of telepathy, the idea was for Lesley to receive a randomly selected line from a book whilst being submersed under twelve feet of water and miles from the London Piccadilly studios. She would be accompanied by a professional diver for safety, but he would also act as a judge representing the eyes of the listening audience. His name was Stanley Mearns, a well-known and respected diving training instructor who operated out of the Surrey test centre.

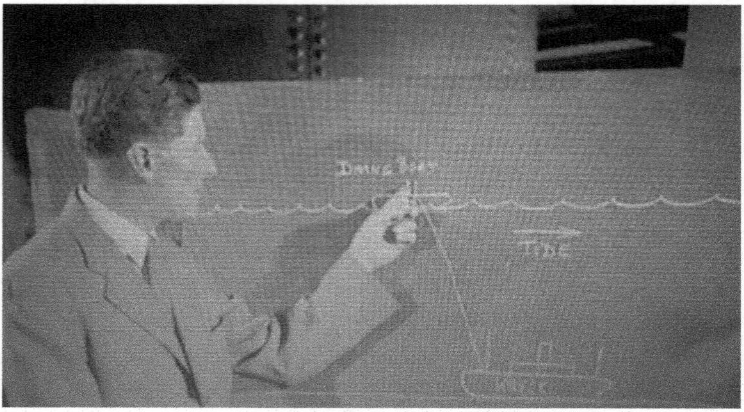

Diving Instructor Stanley Mearns

Lesley was in good hands and Stanley enjoyed her company. He would joke to colleagues about how lucky he was to be with the famous Lesley in a tight secluded close quarter that was the bell. He was a handsome man who felt gallant and proud of the responsibility entrusted to him. It was unusual for non-divers to be using the facilities, let-alone the famous, and Stanley felt privileged to be a part of the proceedings.

Back in the Piccadilly studios in London were two other judges. They were also to be the eyes of the listening audience. Their job was to ensure all was true and fair and that there could be no cheating going on behind the BBC microphones in the studio. They were actress, Rosamund John and the novelist, playwright, screenwriter and director, Noel Langley.

Rosamund John

Rosamund John was one of Britain's most popular film actresses of the forties. She was voted second only to Margaret Lockwood as the country's favourite British female star in 1944. Among her films were two of the finest of the decade, The Way to the Stars and Green for Danger.

Noel Langley

Judge number two, Noel Langley was born Christmas day in the year 1911 and was originally a South African citizen (later naturalised American) He was a well-known novelist, playwright, screenwriter and director. He wrote among others, 'Cage Me a Peacock', a satire set in ancient Rome, 'There's a Porpoise Close behind us', and a children's book, 'The Land of Green Ginger'. He is also credited as being one of the screenwriters for the 1939 film hit, 'The Wizard of Oz'

Both Rosamund John and Noel Langley were upstanding judges with every intention of ensuring all was fair and true during this broadcast. In fact, Rosamund John was intrigued to the point of going that extra mile to seek out the secrets behind this magic. She was a sceptic who did not believe in telepathy, but a lover of pretend, if only she could spy how the pretending was achieved. Prior to attending the Piccadilly studio for the broadcast she was working in Hammersmith, London, on a new film '*She shall have murder*'. Co-actors made suggestions to her about what to look out for. Amongst many theories, she was told to watch Sydney Piddington's hands, as there was probably a secret Morse code device that worked by throbbing or pulsing. Rosamund was convinced this could be the key to it all; however, she quickly dismissed this idea as any throbbing activity would be heard through the microphone itself.

Another theory offered to her too was to examine carefully the way the blackboard was used. It was suggested that the chalk would sound different on it depending where on the board it was being used, thus a list of choices could each sit upon a different part of the structure delivering separate tapping or sliding sounds. Again, this was far from the truth.

Working the grid for this broadcast was my Nan, Rachel Hart, who sat to the right in the front row. Wearing a tan cloth coat and branding a cream handbag, which she sat on her lap, Rachel was all set up to deliver answers to Sydney using the abacus system.

The first test was on the theme of football. You will notice the order of the teams in the list are deliberately placed to assist Sydney in recalling which number represents which team. All Sydney needed to do was assign a meaning to each beginning letter of each team. He did this by inventing this clever memory aid, a question sentence. ***Can We Please Have The Scores?*** =

1.**C**helsea 2.**W**atford 3.**P**ortsmouth 4.**H**ull 5.**T**ottenham 6.**S**wansea.

The Football Test:

Six football teams were selected for the show by W Barrington Dalby, real name William Henry Dalby, a known sports commentator and former boxing referee. The football team names were written as a list on the blackboard, which was positioned at the rear of the platform to the right.

The teams were:

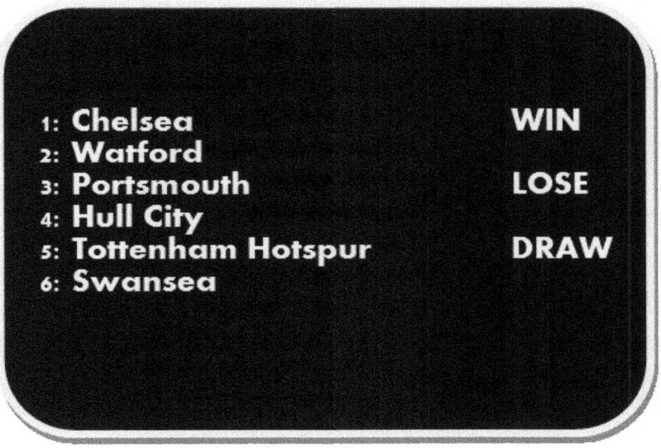

Written to the side of this list were the options WIN, LOSE or DRAW. The idea was for the judge Noel Langley to choose any team he liked by placing a tick next to their name. Sydney would ask the audience to concentrate on his choice and by using 'mass' concentration, pick-up in his mind what team had been picked. Following this, Noel would be asked to choose a second team, the team to play against his first choice, and again Sydney would ask for 'mass' concentration to identify that choice. Finally, Noel was to decide on the outcome of the imaginary football match by choosing one of three results, 'win', 'lose' or 'draw'. Again Sydney would use the forces brought on by 'mass' concentration to discover what the selection was.

The Method:

For this demonstration, Piddington used his ‘abacas’ code. Rachel's hand was naturally hung over her handbag as if holding onto it as it sat guarded on her lap. The code was simple. A hand with all fingers separated represented the first choice in the list - or number 'one'. If two fingers were touching but the others separated, the second choice was indicated. The same followed for three touching fingers, four touching fingers and if all fingers were touching, the fifth choice was indicated. To indicate the sixth choice, all fingers were bent under to form a loose fist. This was another natural looking position for the hand. All of these moves were undetectable to anyone who didn't know the code, or that a code was in action, because the moves looked so natural. The results, 'win' 'lose' or 'draw' were also defined by the numbers 'one' 'two' and 'three'.

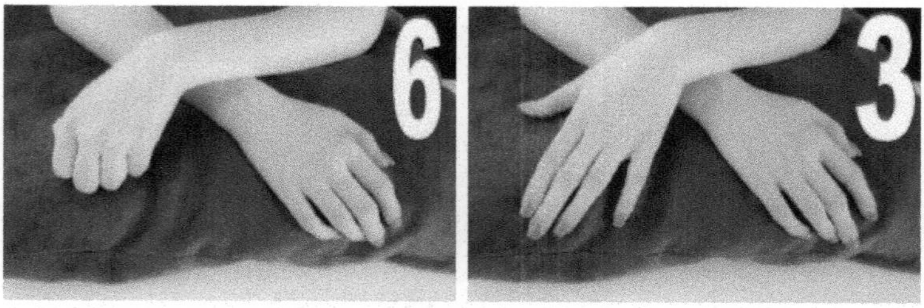

Abacus showing the numbers 6 and 3

Sydney memorised the position of each team using his developed memory system technique, he explains this in an interview on Australian radio. The interview was recorded by ABC’s Kathy Gollan in 1982 but was only discovered in the ABC Archives after a documentary about the Piddingtons, 'Keep Them Guessing', went to air. (See page 64).

For the football team demonstration, Sydney asked Rosamund John to come and blindfold him over by the correctly positioned microphone. From this particular microphone and raised up on the platform, Sydney could comfortably see Rachel Hart's hands by looking downward of the blindfold, through the open gap created by the nose, a technique well known to magicians of today.

Determined to ensure Sydney could not see, Rosamund wrapped the white handkerchief over his eyes and tied it so tight it literally hurt him. It also dislodged the positioning of the blindfold to a point clearly observed by Stephen Grenfell that Sydney could see through the bottom of it and Stephen made mention of it on the air. However, he quickly remarked that this was acceptable as Piddington would have his back to the blackboard. Sydney reacted to this interlude by adjusting his blindfold as he still wished to maintain the idea that a blindfold meant that he could not see.

Sydney gestured Rosamund John to guide his hand toward the microphone, thus giving her the false impression he could not see anything and felt insecure on the platform. Rosamund took his left hand and kept hold of it throughout the demonstration because she wanted to discount the idea a throbbing Morse code device was in action somewhere. To her amazement, Sydney still managed to conclude the correct answers. However, she wasn't through with attempting to discover the trick. It was her turn to choose two teams, which Sydney correctly identified. Next she was asked to choose the result of the imaginary football game by putting a tick next to any of the words 'win', 'lose' or 'draw'. Rosamund deliberately kept her chalk silent by very lightly marking her choice. This made it difficult for grid operator Rachel Hart to see her choice once her hand had withdrawn from the blackboard. Where other chalk markings had been rubbed out to prepare for Rosamund's random selections, the blackboard was peppered with light smudges and chalk markings. Rachel Hart had no idea what she actually picked. In this instance, the signal for 'I don't know' was given by naturally linking both hands together and interlocking the fingers. Sydney had no choice but to guess the result of the imaginary Chelsea 'v' Swansea game. He said it was a 'win', but got it wrong. He just apologised and moved on. He wasn't too concerned because an error only added more authenticity to the idea telepathy was at play.

The Diving Bell Book Test:

Next it was time to return to Lesley in the diving training and test centre in Surbiton, where commentator Gilbert Harding was on the microphone to detail the next step in the diving bell telepathy test. He explained that Lesley was to enter the diving bell and be submerged under twelve feet of water, where she would then attempt to receive a line of print, taken from a book that was back in the Piccadilly studio. He emphasised that it was a line she had never seen before, from a book she had never seen before.

The book used was provided by the BBC. It was sealed in wrapping paper and tied with thick string, thus to ensure no one could have seen the book prior to the test. Studio commentator, Stephen Grenfell next explained that all contact with the Surbiton diving test centre would be cut to ensure that no one down there could hear anything that happened in the Piccadilly studio. And sure enough, communications were truly cut. Lesley was out of contact and submerged inside a diving bell under twelve feet of heavy tank water.

Meanwhile, back in London, the task to unwrap the book and randomly select a page number and then a line, in a manner that was fair and true, was to commence.

Sydney asked judge Noel Langley if he received a package given to him by the BBC. Noel confirms he had. Sydney asks him if he knows what the book is or if anyone else, he is aware of, could know what the book is, and Noel says;

'*As far as I know, nobody in this studio knows, it is very well sealed*!'

Sydney asks Noel to break open the package containing the book. Using a razor blade he slices through the thick string and eventually removes the thick paper covering it. Next he is asked to reveal the title of the book.

"*The Life of Benjamin Disraeli* (volume 1 1804 1859) *by William Flavelle Monypenny and George Earle Buckle*." announced Noel.

Next Noel is asked to reveal the number of pages it has. He says it has 1668 pages. Sydney then asks him to examine the book to ensure it is a real book and is not strange in any way. While Noel is undertaking his task and checking the book, an item he is very familiar with, Sydney sets about collecting a random page number.

Generating a randomised page number:

Sydney Piddington has to be recognised for the genius he truly was by this cunningly simple but virtually undetectable page force. Taking hold of a pad of paper and a pencil, Sydney asks Rosamund to write any single digit number on his pad and sign her initials next to it. He then enters the studio audience. He approaches random people and asks them to write a single digit number on the pad, placing their initials next to the figure so it can be referenced back to them later if need-be. The next person also writes a single digit number on the pad, placing their choice underneath the first number so it can be added up later. Several others are asked to write any single number on the pad until the last person is asked to add up all the numbers.

The total is around '35'. As the book has 1668 pages, the chosen mathematician of the audience is asked to either, leave the total at '35' or bring the total into the 'hundreds' bracket by prefixing any number between 1 and 16 in front of the current total of '35'. She does so by adding a '7' bringing the total to '735'. Now the judges are asked to turn to page '735' and use the last digit of the total, '5' as a guide to the line to be used. The judges now navigate to page '735' and countdown to line number '5' where the line reads; "*...waited a day for Stanley's ultimatum, and then told...*"

It is now pointed out in summary that no pad switch took place and all the figures on the pad are initialled by all the contributors. This is absolutely true.

Sydney asked Rosamund John if she was satisfied that all the figures are the ones provided by the audience. She said *'Yes quite satisfied'*. Sydney also asked Noel Langley if he was satisfied the volume he looked through was a perfectly ordinary one, and he said he was completely satisfied it was ordinary.

Rosamund John was tasked with identifying the selected line and asked to write the line up on the blackboard for the audience to see. This action also acted to commit the line thus it could not be changed.

Next, Sydney asks Noel Langley if he was given some questions to read out to Gilbert Harding at the diving centre in Surbiton, who would then ask them of Stanley Mearns in the diving bell. Noel refreshes his memory of it and searches for the written questions in his jacket pocket. He finds them. Sydney then required that he asked the questions in any order and used his own words when asking the questions so as not to be accused of delivering a spoken code to Lesley via Gilbert Harding.

The questions were as follows: "*Do you know which book was chosen for this test?*" and "*Has any title or quotation from any book been mentioned in your presence from the studio?*"

Contact was then re-established with Gilbert Harding who relayed the questions to Stanley Mearns who said he did not know of the book and there had been no communication from outside of the diving bell. Gilbert Harding confirmed this. Next Lesley asked for concentration and began to unpick the thoughts she was receiving from Sydney. She settled on the line being;

"*...waiting all day for Stanley's ultimatum and then said...*"

Stephen Grenfell then summarised what had just taken place and re-established that the book was provided by the BBC and Lesley was twelve miles away in Surbiton.

The Method:

So, how did Sydney 'transfer' page '735' and line '5' to Lesley? Of course, as we now know, Lesley already knew the line in advance and just needed to deliver it in a manner fitting that of someone receiving a telepathic communication. Though it was suspected that Lesley knew the line, the illusion itself is truly spectacular and relies on the work of several elements.

To begin with we must remember who the BBC production manager is, the one and only Ian C Messiter. *(See how he operates in the Stratocruiser broadcast).* The book was given to the test by him, so it could be said with sincerity that the BBC truly did provide the book. Ian Messiter was a good personal friend to the Piddingtons. Once Sydney had finished with the book, he returned it to Ian and Ian would simply conveyance the book to Noel Langley to legitimise the source from which the title came.

When looking for a book to use in this show Sydney wanted a big one. Ian Messiter was well placed to find one because, at the time he was also very involved in research for various game shows, new and proposed, thus questions and trivia material came in the form of books, many books. One of these books was –'*The Life of Benjamin Disraeli* – Volume 1.'

Choosing the line was even simpler. Instead of looking through the 1638 pages for a suitable line, Lesley just opened the book in the middle and pointed to a line. She would learn the line by writing it down three times on a piece of paper and then forming a mental image that would remind her of "*waited all day for Stanley's ultimatum and then told...*" It was pure luck that her diving bell companion was called Stanley, although a very common name at the time.

Now the book, the page and the line had been chosen, it was down to Sydney to force the location of the line onto the unsuspecting nation, without being caught doing so. This was a show listened to by nearly 20 million people and they included many scientists who took a close interest in the study of Telepathy. There were also many conjurers out there, many with knowledge about how to force choices in a seemingly randomised way. Sydney knew exactly how to do it; he would invent his own method, a system unknown thus far and one that could not be clearly seen. My Uncle, Dave Daye was taught this method during a rehearsal at the house.

The Background:

The story goes like this; Sydney was looking for a method using mathematics that would force a total in an unsuspecting way. He looked at several known systems that he might adapt and hide from the knowledgeable, but with each formula came an obvious-ability that just sent it to the bin. The system needed to seem fair. Adding randomly collected numbers seemed fair enough, especially if the numbers were truly random. The problem now was how to steer these random choices to meet the total he desired. After some thought, Sydney realised he would need a secret 'tool' to ensure the desired total would always be equalled, yet the totals would always be different if the method was repeated. This is how it worked:

Sydney would walk into an audience of strangers with a pad of paper and a pencil. He would ask a random person to write any single figure on his writing pad. He could easily require one of the judges to write the first number to strengthen the fact it is truly random, and sometimes he did. He would approach another random person and ask him or her to write any single number under the last one to create a sum. For added effect, he would ask each person to identify their chosen number by placing their initials at the side. With two numbers on the pad Sydney asked for a third.

So at this point let me tell you that Sydney is adding these numbers as they come. He knows the total so far. If he wants to ensure the total is '35' he will stop asking for random numbers at the point another number could over-shoot the desired total. For example 7 + 9 + 4 + 8 + STOP because if the next random number is higher than a '7' the force is void. At this point, Sydney knows it must be a number '7' that is written next, so he turns to his 'tool', otherwise called a 'secret assistant' who sits in the audience and who will also calculate the current total and add the desired number '7'. The total is now '35'. On this show the same person is asked to add up the numbers. This is so the 'tool' can ensure he has good time to correctly insert the right missing figure and if there are any errors doing so, he can still derive the total to be '35' as a last resort. Next Sydney turns to a second secret assistant and requests her to bring the total up into the 'hundreds' bracket by adding a prefix to the total. The secret assistant does so thus cunningly bringing the total to equal the predetermined page number '735'. The line to be used is simply determined by the last digit of the total, which at this point looks fairly and truly random.

After summarising the process to show that all was fair, Lesley seemingly received the line as a thought message, unpicking its words and then assembling them into a coherent order.

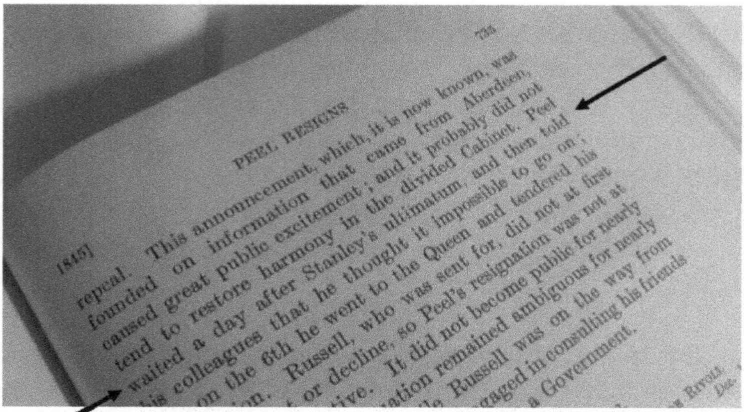
PEEL RESIGNS 735

[1845] repeal. This announcement, which, it is now known, was founded on information that came from Aberdeen, caused great public excitement; and it probably did not tend to restore harmony in the divided Cabinet. Peel waited a day after Stanley's ultimatum, and then told his colleagues that he thought it impossible to go on; on the 6th he went to the Queen and tendered his

Russell, who was sent for, did not at first

or decline, so Peel's resignation was not at

It did not become public for nearly

remained ambiguous for nearly

Russell was on the way from

gaged in consulting his friends

a Government.

Page 735 line 5. The life of Benjamin Disraeli. Vol. 1.

Sydney named his system 'the icing on the cake' and referred to it that way. He would say something like, "we will do a book test and use the icing on the cake". This was a good example of how Sydney visualised the world around him, bringing a brand new world into existence inside his mind. The sponge of the cake was the true part. It was a sponge cake. However, now the shape was formed he could put icing on top and create any theme he chose. It would always still be a sponge cake, but no one would ever know once he decorated it. Collecting the truly random numbers in his force was like making the sponge; all the hard work was done. There was the cake, it was ready to eat. It had flavour and shape. When he turned to the 'tools' hidden amongst his audience, he was just ensuring he ended up with the right result, he was simply adding the 'icing' to his sponge cake and turning it into a birthday cake, or a wedding cake, or a new-born child cake, or any cake, any total he required. In the case of the diving bell thought transference effect his cake looked exactly like the number '735' after he had iced it.

6 MURDER BROADCAST

. . .

2nd show of series 2 1949

Taking you back in time to August 1949 and both Sydney and Lesley are together in the number one Piccadilly studio broadcasting their show. The British nation, now glued to their radio sets in their millions, are poised to be amazed. By now the Piddingtons are the talk of the land with a galaxy of newspapers reporting on their controversial abilities. This continued into the following year and it soon became a journalist's dream to catch them out and claim the scoop. In March of 1950, Lionel Hale, the playwright, broadcaster and theatre critic, in a look-back piece, writes in the Spectator about his experience on one of the Piddington shows.

GENUINE telepathy or a grave-faced trick? By Lionel Hale. Published 10th March 1950.

Lionel Hale

'I have myself investigated the Piddingtons at close quarters and am little nearer the proof. During one of their broadcasts I was invited to make a short tour of London town with Mrs. Piddington in a taxi-cab, while in the B.B.C.'s Piccadilly studio another independent judge picked out one of ten London theatrical shows written on-a blackboard. About Soho we went, round Trafalgar Square, up the Mall, to the Palace, back along Birdcage Walk. We were, I judged, incommunicado. At Piccadilly Circus Mrs. Piddington (who had preserved a remarkable composure) wrote "Oklahoma!" on a piece of paper and pressed it shyly into my hand. And when we returned to the studio, "Oklahoma!" was right. Now, of course, it may be that this title was, say, fourth on the blackboard list, and that some ingenious code had been evolved, maybe they had four street-barrows hastily mustered in; or, the hand of the Guinness clock at Piccadilly Circus may have been put to four o'clock, or the officer commanding at Wellington Barracks may have served as accomplice and ordered out four Guardsmen to drill on the square. This solution would argue, however, some delicate diplomacy in arrangement; and Mrs. Piddington anyway appeared to be enjoying the refreshing slumbers of youth, with her eyes closed, throughout. In later broadcasts she graduated from my taxi-cab to a diving-bell in the Staines reservoir and an aeroplane flying over Bristol with equal success.

Mr. Braddon, the manager of the charming Piddington act, does very little to solve the controversy. True, he scoffs heartily and good-humouredly at the disbelievers; but it is important to note that he not once explicitly and flatly comes out with the claim, "This is telepathy and no trick." It was he, a fellow-prisoner-of-war with Mr. Piddington in the Changi camp at Singapore, who first worked out the telepathy act with him; and in the circumstances perhaps he would not wish to lay claim to the status of an impartial seeker after truth. But to review the telepathy issue is to blow on somewhat cold ashes; and a great part of Mr. Braddon's book concerns itself with Mr. Piddington's career as an Australian soldier In the Malayan campaign or as a prisoner-of-war in Japanese hands. The chapters here are written with a tough kind of humour: the captivity which Mr. Braddon shared with Mr. Piddington is drawn with excellent energy, and the book revives our admiration for the men who endured torture and starvation so long and with so salty a stoicism. Mr. Braddon continues on to post-war Australia, the meeting and marriage of the Piddingtons, and their joint adventurous career in front of microphones and audience; he presents a young couple with their hearts in the right place and their heads firmly screwed on. Two facts emerge from the narrative which, taken jointly, might have a bearing on the telepathy controversy. Firstly, Sydney

Piddington was an amateur conjurer. Secondly, Lesley Piddington was a professional actress.'

The Broadcast:

In this live broadcast, the second broadcast of the second series of three shows, the Piddingtons plan to prove many of the theorists wrong. Letters to the BBC from critics offering techniques about how they did their tricks were arriving in droves. Some of the letters were aggressive while others polite. It seemed to the Piddingtons that this was a battle of wits between them and the theorists rather than a piece of entertainment designed to cause conversations, stimulate minds and add some fun to the radio diet. The BBC, although keen for high ratings, wished to avoid any road leading to complaints. The science community rippled the waters with some objections, generally stating that the study of telepathy was a serious one and should not be staged for entertainment purposes but investigated in properly funded laboratory conditions. Letters were written inviting the Piddingtons to undergo tests, thus proving their psychic abilities under proper controls. Frustratingly, the Piddingtons never claimed they ever possessed special abilities in this phenomena, thus the idea they had made such claims were wrongly concluded by the science community themselves. On the other hand, the Piddingtons never admitted they *didn't* possess special abilities in extra sensory perception. This was a 'first' for an act of this type.

The Piddingtons wanted there to be three well known and trusted judges on this particular show; people who were unlikely to be doubted, not that they ever were. Sydney had some convincing tests to demonstrate, tests that would silence many of the critics' once-and-for-all. Ian Messiter, in charge of production, invited three big names onto the panel, Duncan Carse, David Tomlinson and Edana Romney.

Actor and celebrity explorer Duncan Carse (1913–2004) was a British explorer and actor known for surveying South Georgia and for the portrayal of Special Agent Dick Barton on BBC Radio.

Duncan Carse

David Tomlinson

David Tomlinson

(7 May 1917 – 24 June 2000) was an English film actor and comedian. He is primarily remembered for his roles as authority figure George Banks in '*Mary Poppins'*,-fraudulent magician Professor Emelius Browne in '*Bedknobs and Broomsticks'* and as hapless antagonist Peter Thorndyke in that comical motorcar farce '*The Love Bug'*.

Edana Romney was born on March 15, 1919 in Johannesburg, South Africa as Edana Rubenstein. She was an actress and writer, known for Corridor of Mirrors (1948), Alibi (1942) and The Strangler (1941).

Edana Romney

With less media entertainment available back then, family games were popular in British culture, and made perfect themes for magic tricks.

The first Test: Murder in the Piccadilly Studios:

This test of telepathy was based upon a parlour game known today as wink murder. The original game played like this; in each round of play, one player is secretly assigned the role of "murderer", perhaps by handing every player a playing card with a particular card signifying that the recipient is the 'murderer'. The murderer has the ability to "kill" other players by making eye contact and winking at them. If a player is winked at, they must count silently to five before feigning sudden death, and either lying on the floor where they died, or silently leaving the playing area.

If a player suspects they know the identity of the murderer, they may raise their hand and announce "I accuse", without naming their suspect. At this point, the game pauses and the accuser asks for somebody to second their accusation, again with neither naming a suspect. When they have a seconder, both of these players simultaneously point to their suspect; if they are both pointing to a player who admits to being the 'murderer', the game ends. Otherwise (if they are pointing to different players or to an innocent player) the accusers are both eliminated as if they had been 'murdered'. Players are forbidden from communicating their thoughts on who the 'murderer' might be, and players who are not the 'murderer' are not allowed to wink.

The objective of the murderer is to 'murder' as many people as possible without being caught.

Sydney adapted the game for the show and it was Lesley's job to play detective and identify, not only the killer, but the victim and the method of murder. Sydney did not wish to have these roles determined by someone winking at people, but instead to remove Lesley from the studio under the guard of a judge and return her after the selections had been decided. Adana Romney was asked to escort Lesley out of the studio to an area where nothing from the number 'one' studio could be seen or heard.

Meanwhile, inside, Duncan Carse, already well known as a hero special agent, was charged with choosing a member of the audience to play the victim, another to play the murderer and then decide upon the method used to commit the crime. Looking out over the 200 strong audience from the platform for the victim, Duncan pointed to a man in the 7th row, (3 rows from the back of the studio) who sat in the aisle seat (first seat on the row). Next he pointed to the murderer, a woman who was sat in the 4th row, again in the aisle seat. After an imaginative thought, he decided that the method was thus; the killer used a hammer to crown her victim, drive him to a big sewer and dump him in.

The stage was set, the killer, her victim and how she killed him had been decided. Sydney announced he would remove himself to a secluded place behind a screen partition so it would not be possible for him to communicate in code to Lesley when she returned. He left the stage. Lesley was brought back into the studio with Adana Romney still guarding her. Adana was asked two 'check' questions to verify Lesley did not see or hear anything while outside the studio. Adana confirmed Lesley had not seen or heard anything. Lesley then asked the audience to concentrate on who the victim was. She picked up a hand-held BBC microphone and entered the audience. She followed her psychic abilities to the 7th row and pointed to the victim chosen by Duncan. Lesley then returned to the platform and again asked for concentration from the audience. Again she entered the audience. She went to the 4th row and pointed to the murderer sat in the first seat. Once again she returned to the platform and took a breath. It was time to identify the method used to kill the victim. After asking for mass concentration she picked out that the victim had been struck several times, the other details were not mentioned, however she was correct. The applause ended the demonstration and Sydney returned to the platform.

This simple piece of deduction was very much perceived by the audience as an example of Lesley being guided by telepathic thoughts from Sydney, to correctly identify three separate options, chosen fairly by Judge Duncan Carse. The selection was truly random and could have involved any members of the audience. Of course, there was no telepathic ability involved in this trick at all. Once again Lesley worked from the Grid Operator who was sat in the front row. On this occasion it was George Hart pointing the fingers and spelling out the word 'strike'. But it is how George was able to store this information without getting up, turning around and recording the positions himself, that is the clever part. To explain how the operation worked I need to rewind the trick and take you back to the part after the choices had been made by Duncan Carse.

Sydney has an important part to play in informing George of the exact information to pass to Lesley. He does this by summarising all the choices made. This is what he actually says in the broadcast;

"That sounds delightful. That's our victim on the right hand side, the 7th row back, the first person. Our Murderess, on the left hand side, 4 rows back and the first. And you are, I understand, going to STRIKE this man, are you, until he's unconscious with a hammer? That's very pleasant indeed..."

It is in this verbal verification of the facts where grid operator George obtains his information. To deliver the information to Lesley is done in two parts. First George indicates the row is number 7. This is done using Piddington's abacus system. *(See page 84)*. The left and right side of the aisle, taken from the point-of-view of the platform, was indicated simply by pointing the right foot right and leaving the left foot facing forward. This said, the intricacy of the delivery of information uses another clever diversion too, the need to ask 'check' questions. David Tomlinson was charged with asking Miss Romney two 'check' questions. He was told to ask them in any order so as to eliminate any idea the questions contained any covert codes.

"Have you been with Lesley all the time?"
"While you were outside did you see or hear anything that was happening in this studio?"

To the audience it seemed the questions were to confirm Lesley had not seen or heard anything from the studio, thus she could not know of the choices made. And, yes, this was true. In fact, this 'check' questioning was also a clever way of allowing George Hart more time to communicate the grid references to Lesley. By the time the questions were done, all Lesley had to do was ask for concentration and she was off. There was no need for Lesley to stand on that platform any longer than a few seconds, so it seemed. It was quickly forgotten that 54 seconds had already passed before Lesley was handed the limelight under which to play her part. This is known in the magic trade as ‘time misdirection’.

Of course Lesley identifies the 'corpse' correctly. She then needs to return to the platform to obtain the second set of grid references, which can only be observed from the platform position. This is why Lesley always returns to the platform instead of moving onto find her second target while down in the aisle. Once the two targets had been correctly pointed out by Lesley she now had to name the method by which the murder was achieved. Remember Sydney's summing up of the choices was done to feed George with the necessary information to pass to Lesley, and part of that information detailed a description of the murder method, which used the word 'STRIKE', meaning 'struck by an object'. George waited for Lesley's cue word, 'concentrate', before spelling out the word 'strike' on the grid.

Lesley could read the grid as if reading a ticker-tape machine, the method taught to her by Sydney back on Bondi Beach. He would use the sand as a blackboard to demonstrate the technique. This involves absorbing one letter at a time while pronouncing the sound of the word in real time as the letters appear as opposed to gathering the letters and afterwards, looking at the sequence of letters to identify the word. Lesley was well rehearsed in this technique by now and it was easy for her to read the fingering, visualise the grid, see the letter and sound it out in silence.

S T R I K E = (4.4) - (4.5) - (4.3) - (2.4) - (3.1) – (1.5)

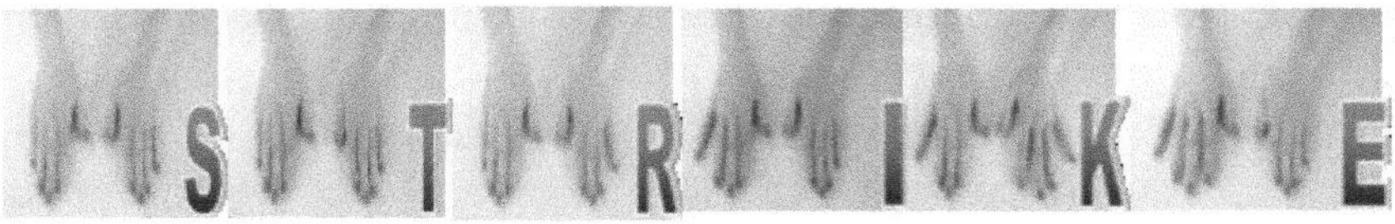

In this broadcast, Lesley issued the code word 'concentrate' and George began spelling out the word 'strike'. Lesley was able to watch the letters appear while still managing to instruct the audience to concentrate on the way the 'nasty female' put away her victim. Lesley was well practised in reading the ‘grid’ by now. However, the arduous task of reading the grid while talking does slow Lesley down and in the broadcast, she can be heard struggling to create a flow in her sentences. Lesley delivered her verdict by suggesting the method involved 'striking' at the victim. A pause was heard causing her to seek approval of her answer. She was correct enough; although it is obvious the word 'hammer' would have been better. This was discussed afterwards but as George was given the word 'strike' by Sydney, who had introduced the word into the mix during his summary that was the word he delivered. It was decided by Lesley that the effect had lost some impact because the key-word was in fact 'hammer' and perhaps in future the key-word should always be used. Sydney argued that 'hammer' was too vague and that a clearer alternative was better. He joked that Lesley may have jumped in too early and accuse the murderer of killing her victim with a Ham joint. Also the broadcast was running to a strict time limit that put limitations on how long they could spend on one item in the show. Lesley argued that there was plenty of time to use the word 'hammer' it has the same number of letters as ‘strike’ and she disagreed with conviction. Sydney explained that he always tells his audiences he will try to transmit an 'idea' of the word or object in play, and not that he will transmit an exact copy of it. Here he was supposed to be transmitting an ‘action’. This ‘idea’ allows Lesley to claim success even if the results are not exact; it adds legitimacy to the demonstration and offers a way-out if ever mistakes occur. The Piddingtons had a small falling out over their differing opinions on the matter which led them to listen back to the broadcast. This was exactly what they did, but it was without the corporation's consent. A BBC employee, who should remain anonymous, illegally copied as many recordings as he could onto vinyl. This proved to be a valuable reference tool for Sydney, and it allowed him to further improve his demonstrations.

The Piddingtons Separate:

In the next demonstration of thought transference Sydney explains that Lesley would be taken to a separate sound-proof studio where she would be totally isolated with no means of hearing anything happening in the main studio. From there she would wait until the exact moment, the exact second, she received a transmission from Sydney's mind, and then speak what she received. To achieve this, judges are asked to think of any word or an object and then decide on when Sydney should begin to transmit it to Lesley. This would demonstrate that thought transference between the two is genuinely occurring as Lesley would only react at the time determined by the judge. They can choose that Sydney waits 10 seconds, 23 seconds, 30 seconds or any number of seconds before transmitting his thought to Lesley. Commentator, Stephen Grenfell, using a stopwatch, would count down to zero the allocated time frame and then see if Lesley receives a thought on that pre-determined second. If she does, she would begin to describe what she is seeing in her mind.

The sound proof studio had been checked by David Tomlinson who confirmed the studio is without means to hear anything outside of it. He then escorts Lesley to it, stands outside and guards the door to ensure no one can get to her. A window between the engineer’s gallery and the studio is covered to stop any visual codes being communicated.

Meanwhile, back in the main studio Sydney asks Edana Romney to nominate any word or object, something easily visualised rather than abstract. Romney looks at her pearl ring and says she is choosing it to be the object Lesley must receive. She asks that 30 seconds pass before Sydney transmits the ring to his wife and she even starts the count at a moment of her own choosing. Grenfell counts down from 30 seconds to zero and on zero, Lesley begins to talk. She slowly gathers the image of a ring and that it belongs to Edana Romney.

Next Duncan Carse takes a turn and chooses a Penguin. He asks for 25 seconds to pass before Sydney transmits the thought of it. Lesley comes in on cue and slowly arrives at the correct answer, mentioning also who made the choice.

For the third part of the demonstration, Sydney calls for a random member of the audience to join the test and insert an extra word into a sentence both Edana and Duncan make up. The idea was that Sydney would then transmit the 'idea' of the complete sentence to Lesley. The judges are also given responsibility of choosing the audience member, thus proving the spectator is fairly chosen and is not a confederate.

Unfortunately, Edana chose a lady in the front row who, unknown to her, was actually Ian Messiter's wife. Ian being the production manager for the Piddington series. Her name was Enid, née Senior and at first she did not object to joining the test. She stood to join them. However, Ian Messiter motioned to Sydney, who also knew what had just happened, not to use her. Sydney quickly muscled in to stop the choice and explained that he had just been informed that the lady was Ian Messiter's wife and people may consider her a confederate. Sydney suggested a different person was chosen. Enid retook her seat smiling with a quiet blush. It was never noticed that the communication from Ian to Sydney was never heard on the live show, suggesting a silent 'nod' of disapproval was given which Sydney understood. Thus concluding he knew this was Ian's wife without being told of it.

This was down played as a comical mistake that was no fault of the judges. Sydney simply laughed it off and moved things forward. It also pleased Sydney, greatly, because it was unscripted powerful proof that the judges were true and fair, hence such an error could come to pass in the first place. This was superb for the trick, adding another blow to the theory that confederates were ever used in his act. However Sydney wanted to play on it further and he asked if anyone wanted to change the person chosen from the audience, but all were happy with the choice.

Once the stage was set for the next part of the demonstration, Edana came out with a sentence she had just that moment thought of. It was; “Darling I love you”. She looked at Duncan Carse as she said it which caused a titter. The chosen audience spectator added the word “Tremendously” at the end of the sentence. Her name was Kitty McKay and she was an employee for the then up-coming company Littlewoods. She commented later that she was not happy with her chosen word or the way she sounded when she said it.

Now Sydney had a sentence only just created and a 'check word' as he called it, from a completely random member of the audience. All was true and fair and everyone could see that was definitely the case. 30 seconds were given before Sydney was to transmit to Lesley; who was still guarded by David Tomlinson out by the second sound-proof studio.

As expected, on the exact second 'zero', Lesley spoke. She slowly unpicked Sydney's thoughts and delivered the line; “I love you dear, a lot”, which was close enough and convincing enough for all. The applause filled the studio, the airwaves and the Piddington's hearts.

It was time for Sydney to further kill off any idea that Lesley was being fed the answers via any other method other than telepathy. He invented a new trick to achieve this, using a method he had once abandoned. However, in this part of the demonstration such a method was perfect because it would allow them to add bafflement and intrigue the journalists.

With Lesley alone and hearing nothing from the main studio, only speaking at the moment she receives thoughts from Sydney, it was time to throw a 'curve ball' into the mix. Sydney asked Edana to write the name of any playing card on a pad of paper, but not to speak her choice aloud. She was only to show it to him and he would then transmit the card to his wife, again at the chosen moment. This was a clever move because now it was true and fair that only Edana and Sydney held knowledge of the chosen card, and neither of them were anywhere near Lesley. She was still under the guard of David Tomlinson. If Lesley spoke the name of this card at the right moment, it would be miraculous, solid proof of ESP abilities, a big story for the press and a major boost to the listening figures once word-of-mouth worked up an appetite. Once Edana had written her card choice on the pad of paper she showed it to Sydney. This is what was said next;

Sydney: "I will just ask for silence, and once again Lesley will rely entirely on a telepathic **flash** which she will receive from me here. Now Miss Romney, will you just stand by this microphone here, and I want you to concentrate with me on **this**. Thank you".

I ask you to concentrate on Lesley so she will know there was a message to receive. See if you listeners at home can receive it before she does. And now in the studio, your silence please."

Lesley: "It's a diamond, or red court card, I think it's the Jack of Diamonds"

Sydney: "It's a court card Lesley... Oh sorry she can't hear me; it's a court card - the Queen of Hearts. Still, she got the court card and the colour was right. Thank you very much."

So how did the Piddingtons manage to create the illusion that a person isolated inside a soundproof room, with no method of communication into that room, could pick up thoughts transmitted at pre-determined moments in time? Furthermore, the room was open to be inspected by a fair-play judge who was satisfied no method of communication was present. For the answer I will need to take you back in time to Sydney Piddington's POW days in the Changi jail.

During the Second World War, prisoners of war relied upon news broadcasts from the BBC to keep them up to date with the war effort. Radios were not permitted in any POW camp, and that included Changi where Sydney was incarcerated. Being caught listening to a radio was punishable by death and this was a well-known fact of war time life. This meant that to operate a radio was a big risk so it had to be well hidden. A prisoner could not write anything down he heard on the wireless as this was far too dangerous. The 'secret radio' was about the size of a shoe box and it usually had a set of headphones. Sydney Piddington was one of a small group of men who ran a secret radio in the Changi jail. It was hidden in a room used to store concert props and instruments. The BBC broadcast a news bulletin lasting about ten or twelve minutes around midnight Singapore time and Sydney would listen using the headphones. The men knew the radio could never be found, so it was always packed away and hidden well. The aerial was a wire that would run from the set to the drums, where it was fixed. When the radio was hidden, the aerial was left hanging from the drum. It could not be identified as an aerial without the radio; it was just a piece of wire.

With this in mind it is not difficult to see how the Piddingtons thought to use a secret radio inside the soundproof studio. This was why Lesley had to be inside the room alone, and the door guarded under the misapprehension it was to stop anyone getting in. The radio they used was compact and more modern than the one used in the Changi camp; it ran off an internal battery and could be placed inside the room after it had been checked.

This method was ideal because the broadcast was a live one. However, it did offer a small problem for the Piddingtons, that there was a short delay between what was said in the main studio and the broadcast reaching the radio set. It was a delay of about 3 to 4 seconds. This was compensated for by introducing a count-down whereby Lesley would begin receiving the thought transmissions at a pre-determined moment, and this count down also allowed Lesley time to turn the volume down on the radio so it could not be heard in the background when she was on the air. For example; when the countdown in the studio reached 10 seconds, Lesley would exit the headset and begin counting down in her head from the number 7, thus taking into account the time delay. She would then speak what she had secretly heard, through the secret radio, as if she was receiving thoughts.

However, Lesley failed to hide the secret radio completely, as the delayed broadcast can actually be heard where she has failed to turn the volume down enough. Listening carefully, the sound can be heard coming from the headset in certain places during her broadcast with Duncan Carse who chose the word 'Penguin'. Lesley says "Mr Barton has chosen something – An animal? - It's a bird! "And after each statement you can hear the delayed broadcast behind her, albeit faint enough to be missed if you are not listening for it.

The playing card effect

Transmitting the value of the playing card, bearing in mind that Lesley can hear what is happening in the studio via the secret radio, was done using a spoken code that would inform Lesley of the value of the card.

Sydney invented the code while he was in London. It did not exist before then because he did not like to use spoken codes. This was an out-dated method in stage telepathy and one that audiences knew about. In this trick however, the idea that Lesley could not hear what was happening in the number one studio was a perfect distraction from the idea he was using a spoken code.

In later years, confederate and friend Dave Daye acquired the code for his own use. He was a keen player of a card game called 'Kalooki', and he also liked to do a few card tricks too. It also transpired that this was not the only card code invented by Sydney Piddington. He also invented a visual code that was completely silent. This silent code did not use hand signals but a completely new method of playing-card communication that has never been seen before the existence of this book. Until now, all of Sydney Piddington's methods have been completely secret.

He never used the silent card code in his career but it still exists. The visual code was learned by both George and Rachel Hart for the planned theatre tours the Piddingtons were working towards. In those days, there was more money to be made touring with a show than could be made on radio or television.

The word-code used by Sydney on the Murder game broadcast does not appear in the BBC script but was recorded by my grandfather in his RAF notebook. It worked as follows;

(MA = Memory Aid, the best way to remember the key words).

The Playing Card Code:

<u>Sydney says:</u>
"I want you to concentrate with me on... (Insert Key-word that identifies the card value)"

A = This

2 = This choice

3 = This card you have chosen

4 = Your card

5 = Your choice

6 = Your choice of card

7 = The card

8 = The choice

9 = The choice you have made

10 = What you have written down

The values 1, 2 and 3 are in a category preceded by the word 'THIS'.

The values 4, 5 and 6 are in a category preceded by the word 'YOUR'

The values 7, 8 and 9 are in a category preceded by the word 'THE'

The value of '10' is in a category preceded by the word 'WHAT'

If the code word 'FLASH' was given the category using the preceding word 'THIS' now belongs to the 3 Court Cards and are used in exactly the same sequence as in 1, 2 and 3. Except the value of '1' becomes 'Jack. The value of '2' becomes 'Queen' and the value of '3' becomes King.

"FLASH" = Court Card = Picture Card. (MA = Taking a picture uses a flash)

J = This (MA = short word signifies seniority of court card)

Q = This Card (MA = Two words signifies higher seniority of court card)

K = This card you have chosen (Many words signifies highest seniority of court card)

The Suits:

(Indicated after the coded request to concentrate on 'the card' with me, a form of 'thanks' is given).

D = Thank you (MA = After receiving a gift of a diamond)

H = Thank you very much (MA = Heartfelt gratitude)

S = Thanks (MA = The sound of the letter 'S' on the end = 'S' is for 'spades')

C = NO THANKS GIVEN (MA = Cold attitude - a word beginning with the letter 'c' for Clubs)

Ironically Sydney messed up his own playing-card code because he coded the wrong card to Lesley. He should have inserted the key-words "This card" and ended with "Thank you very much". Instead, for the Queen of Hearts he recalled the key-words to be "This" and "Thank you" which is the Jack of Diamonds. However, Sydney concluded that Lesley had indeed enjoyed success because she identified a 'red court card'. Unfortunately, the fact that he had messed up his own code and the feeling of surprise as he realised it, threw him into a quandary, and he spoke directly to Lesley knowing she could really hear him. He quickly realised his error and pretended that he had forgotten that she could not hear him. He laughed this off and corrected himself.

The audience was satisfied that Lesley was close enough identifying the red court card and applauded her success. Commentator Stephen Grenfell closed the show with some verbal credits, but not before reiterating the fair and true conditions the Piddingtons were working within, thus telepathy was surely the conclusion to reach.

Afterwards:

After the broadcast Sydney joined his wife and other colleagues in a local pub near the studios. He was upset because he felt the broadcast had been a disaster with his finale trick losing the impact he desired. He was right, the impact had been lost and the press did not go wild over the final test. Lesley was in the better position because she didn't have to learn Sydney's playing card code. She had it written down on a page of paper she could view whilst isolated, unobserved in the soundproof studio.

- A well-deserved day at home for the Piddingtons -

Sydney and Lesley Piddington at their London home

7 TOWER OF LONDON BROADCAST

• •

3rd show of series 1

Production by Frederick Piffard

"...be abandoned as the electrician said that they would have no current..." is now one of the most famous lines from a book of 1940s literature, thanks to the Piddington's. The line is believed to be from a book titled 'MARQUIS', written by George Millar. In the broadcast the book is selected by guest judge, Sir Herbert Dunnico, who had originally picked a different book from a choice of five available. None of the titles used any gimmickry, as suggested by several critics, and all the judges on the show were legitimate. This single line only existed in one of the five books on offer, thus to choose another book would have never made this sentence famous, because it never would have been heard. So how did Sydney Piddington transmit the line from a randomly chosen book to his wife Lesley, who was in the Tower of London, guarded by two other guest judges who were also legitimate? For the answer to that question, and to truly appreciate the genius of Sydney Piddington, we have to go back to the beginning of the set-up.

After completing two shows from their contracted series of eight broadcasts, by now the Piddingtons were already known for their telepathy act and millions were baffled. Lesley knew that some of their past demonstrations, although brilliant, really would benefit from further publicity. The goal remained fixed that they would tour the country appearing in theatres, because that was where the real money was to be made. This meant that they had to raise the profile of their act even further to ensure generous ticket sales and that demanded something better than they had delivered before. As Lesley elegantly put it herself, "we need something glamorous!" I imagine this moment was like a cliff-hanger at the end of a great soap opera, with a thoughtful pause separating the episodes.

However, to maximise their exposure, the Piddington's had two dilemmas to overcome. Firstly, Lesley had the presence-of-mind to realise that the telepathy, however seemingly impossible, was not enough to keep capturing the media attention.

They had accomplished great performances, but Sydney was dissatisfied. He was continually frustrated by letters from the public suggesting they knew how the tricks were done. One in particular suggested that the book tests were achieved simply by his ability to write the line on a piece of card he had inside his trouser pocket and he would later pass it to Lesley. It was this sort of ignorance that encouraged Sydney to actively prove these theories wrong. He was determined to repeat the book test in a way that excluded any possibility of trickery.

While he was consulting with Russell Braddon on how to successfully accomplish such a test, Lesley was also considering matters from a media point of view - what would generate good coverage if not the trick itself? The answer was the venue, where the trick took place! Her first thought was Buckingham Palace; however, this was quickly dismissed as it would never be allowed. The next best thing, she thought, was the Tower of London. "Bloody brilliant" jerked Sydney as he jumped out of his chair. This took Lesley and Russell by surprise causing her to spill some coffee over her top, a story well remembered by my Grandfather George. It was a yellow wool cardigan with loose pockets and it was one of her favourite items. The coffee stain would be hard to shift.

The Piddington's put their Tower idea to the BBC officials. However, not used to arranging such extravagance in radio broadcasting, the BBC dismissed such lunacy and instead suggested using another area of the Piccadilly studios would be easier to arrange and still achieve a demonstration of long distance thought transference. This was not what the Piddingtons wanted to hear. Broadcasting from the Tower would encourage newspaper interest and prove those theorists wrong once and for all. The public were just starting to talk about them and the controversy was starting to bubble over the big question "was it telepathy or a clever trick?" A well-executed, long distance demonstration would achieve their aims – a touch of glamour and mass publicity. The Piddingtons left the BBC studios and jumped into my great uncle, Dave Daye's, black-taxi cab and went to get a Chinese meal of rice to talk some more.

They decided to find out who owned the Tower of London and seek permission to broadcast the book-test demonstration from there. That same evening they went to the Piccadilly Tube lines, fed shillings to the telephones to call everyone they knew in England. "Who owns the Tower of London?" they asked. Unfortunately they had no joy in finding out. Luck came the following day. The Piddingtons were collected from their dwellings by a member of the BBC television staff called Mike. He picked them up in a sports car to take them to Alexander Palace, the then television studios based in Wood Green North London.

The Piddingtons were bound towards the studio to discuss a television demonstration of their act. On route, they asked Mike if he knew who owned the Tower of London and, as luck would have it, he did. "Colonel Carkeet James" he informed them. Furthermore, he offered to ring him up and suggest the idea on their behalf. The Colonel loved the plan. He explained he had heard the first two broadcasts and knew of the Piddingtons. The BBC later rang him to confirm his permission. The Tower of London was booked.

This book test was to be different. Braddon and Sydney had decided to change the original method of the trick to preclude any criticisms or theoretical ideas about the methods. Firstly, the thought transference would be over a long distance, and Lesley would be under the watchful eye of two legitimate and trusted judges, to be chosen later. This would dispel the myth that Sydney was somehow passing written pieces of paper to Lesley via his trouser pockets. Secondly, there needed to be a choice of books for the spectator to choose from, thus killing the idea a pre-arranged sentence was being forced. The books were to be real and without gimmicks of any kind. Thirdly; the method used to select a page and line number needed to come from audience members and this witnessed by two more judges who were trusted by the public. Such a thorough process would dispel any questioning about the 'telepathy' between the two. They considered the minds of the critics to ensure each and every scenario could be seen as confirmation of the telepathy. By the time both were satisfied the system of events was right, London was already asleep and a tired Russell banished to sleep in an armchair until morning.

The search was on for four trusted and distinguished judges, two for Sydney in the Piccadilly studio and two to guard Lesley in the Tower of London. These were:

Rev Sir Herbert Dunnico, born 2nd December 1875); Dunnico was a British Baptist minister, leading Freemason and Labour Party politician.

He was knighted in the New Year Honours 1938, "for political and public services". In 1949 he was very well known to the British public as a distinguished and trustworthy man, thus perfect to appear with the Piddingtons as a fair-play judge.

Dennis Price

The famous actor Dennis Price, born as Dennistoun Franklyn John Rose-Price. He studied acting at the Embassy Theatre School of Acting. Later, he appeared in both theatre productions and film roles, including '*A Canterbury Tale*' (1944).'

These two judges would remain in the Piccadilly studio to watch over Sydney on behalf of listeners. They were also to take part and make choices of their own, all unrehearsed and fair.

Hugh Ross Williamson

To watch over Lesley in the Bloody Tower, would be Hugh Ross Williamson (1901-1978), he was a prolific British historian, and a dramatist.

Starting from a career in the literary world, and having a nonconformist background, he became an Anglican priest in 1943. A priest as distinguished as Williamson was perfect to be a judge on the show.

The final judge was Captain Taprell Dorling, born Taprell 8th September 1883. He served many years in the Navy and on retiring from service, established himself as a popular writer on ships and the sea and on life in the Royal Navy in war and peace.

The Tower Broadcast:

The Piddingtons had four very strong judges for the broadcast and a venue that would entice the media to write about their stunt. Sydney and Russell were about to demonstrate one of the most convincing book-tests ever seen in the history of magic.

The broadcast would run for half an hour but the book test would only run for approximately eight minutes, so Sydney needed to demonstrate some other tests, without Lesley.

Russell made the suggestion that he could take Lesley's place in a test they secretly called the 'Abacus' trick. This was a numbers effect where three 3 digit numbers were written on a blackboard while he was out of the room. The numbers were then added together to find a random total he would then receive as a thought message. He would also identify who wrote which 3 digit number and in which order. Sydney agreed. It was an effect invented by them while in the Changi POW camp, and one that worked well.

Two hundred audience members piled into the Piccadilly studios and took their seats. Lesley and all four judges were there. Once the audience was settled it was announced that the Captain and Williamson would escort Lesley to the Tower of London to guard her during a new test of telepathy. They would ensure that no trickery was in play, that no person would be feeding Lesley any information and moreover, nothing could be heard from the Piccadilly studios that could be deemed as revealing. Lesley and the judges left the studios and ventured to the Tower by car.

The BBC commentator on the broadcast was Colin Wills, a journalist, author and broadcaster.

Colin Wills' voice opened the show by explaining that Sydney would be attempting a new experiment with mass thought transference. The truth behind this was that Piddington had spent so long perfecting the new book-test, he found himself left with time to fill but no real grand trick to fill the empty space with. The tests in the show included a random choices test where judge Sir Herbert Dunnico, while in a separate sound-proof studio, would pick three movie star photos which Sydney would then deliberate on and call each photo correctly; the 'Abacus' effect would follow with Russell Braddon, being introduced as a guest.

The grand finale would be the new book test. The three tests were allocated timings and there was a gap of three minutes still to fill, a long time on radio, so Sydney inserted a non-magical piece called the 'Colours Test'. This invited the listener to receive a thought message themselves, by identifying one of five colours chosen by one of the judges in the studio. Sydney explained that they could receive an impression of the chosen colour he was transmitting over the radio and that a difference of opinion between family members was normal. The chosen colour would be revealed the following week, those who got it right would be deemed gifted like he was. It was satisfactory as a time filler, but more of an entertainment piece than anything magical.

The Herbert Dunnico photos test

Actor Dennis Price was invited to bring with him a packet of film star photographs. Price arrived with 12 photographs. The idea was that Sir Herbert Dunnico, in a sound-proof studio, would choose any of the photographs, naming the star aloud so only an assistant in the main studio could hear his choice through a set of headphones. The assistant would then hold up the relevant printed card to allow the studio audience to see Dunnico's choice. Sydney, blindfolded and with his back to the assistant, would ask the audience to concentrate on the name of the film star so he could name it. Dunnico made three choices and Sydney correctly identified each one.

This was an excellent piece of misdirection because commentator Colin Wills announced that Sir Dennis Price had been invited to bring a packet of film stars to the show, which was true, thus giving the listener the impression that the packet had been unseen until the test. Clever, but not true.

It was essential for Sydney and 'Grid Operator' George Hart, who needed to know who was in the packet, to gain prior knowledge of the list. Sydney needed to memorise his key-cues, which in this instance were the first two letters of the film stars' surname.

Therefore, the printed cards had to be made prior to the test, so the packet was taken off of Price to allow for this. The packet was returned to him afterwards.

It was agreed between George Hart and Sydney that any of the film stars could be identified by just their surnames because each was famous to Piddington, and by showing only the first two letters of that surname he could easily recall the complete name. It was like recalling a well-known modern movie star of today, let's say, the late great Robin Williams. The letters 'W' and 'I' is all that is needed to identify the name of the star within the limited list of 12. If Sydney ever needed George to repeat the letters he would just ask the audience to 'concentrate' or he would say "more intently", which was the spoken code for "more" letters please, usually requested for added confirmation.

The Abacus Trick:

Next it was time to introduce guest, Russell Braddon, who would demonstrate his own telepathic abilities. It was explained that he and Sydney spent time in the Changi POW camp where, together, they practised thought transference tests. One of these tests involved numbers. Russell, in a brief interview with commentator Colin Wills, explained that he had not worked with Sydney since their days in Changi, and that sometimes the telepathy didn't work, especially when working with Dutch people who would only think in Dutch. Although the interview sounded unscripted, it was in fact scripted. Russell Braddon preferred it that way as he was not much of a performer and felt more confident knowing what he was to say in a live radio broadcast environment. He also refused to wear a blindfold for the trick. Instead the writing on the blackboard would be covered over with a cloth to hide it from him.

The 'Abacus' trick began by Russell being escorted out of the number '1' studio by a member of the audience, who was chosen by Colin Wills. While he was gone, Sydney invited both judges to write a 3 digit number on the blackboard. Dennis Price wrote his number first. Then, Sir Herbert Dunnico was invited to write his 3 digit number underneath or above Dennis Price's number. Sydney asked Dennis Price to choose an audience member to come up onto the platform and write a third 3 digit number underneath, in-between or above the other two numbers. Once all three numbers were on the blackboard, Sir Herbert was charged with drawing a line under them and adding up all the numbers to reach a total.

For this reveal let us assume Dunnico wrote 288, Price 475 and the man from the audience contributed 396 with total being 1,159.

The cloth was placed over the blackboard to hide all the numbers, including the total. Sydney left the platform and was taken to another part of the studio so he could not signal anything to Braddon. Russell Braddon was then called back into the studio where his escort was asked a 'check' question by Sir Herbert Dunnico. This was simply; *"While you were outside with Russell Braddon, did you see or hear anything that happened in this studio?"* The lady escort replied *"Nothing whatsoever, nothing whatsoever!"*

It was now up to Russell Braddon to ask the audience to concentrate on who wrote which number. While standing on the platform in front of a BBC microphone on a stand, facing the audience and with his hand shading his eyes like a baseball cap, he announced that the first number was written by Sir Herbert Dunnico, the second number by Dennis Price and the third number was written by a member of the audience. Then he asked the audience to concentrate on the total of the three sets of figures. He announced he received the numbers 1 and a 5, a 9 and a 2. Here he was mixing the correct order of the numbers by siting the first digit at the end. However, there was no number '2' in the total. He had made a mistake.

Next Braddon asked the audience to concentrate on the correct order of the numbers he had received. He slowly announced that the total was 2,159. No applause came. Braddon asked Colin Wills if he was right. Colin explained that he *"wasn't quite right"* and that the total was actually 1,159. He also announced that he had got the order, in which he named the people, correct. The applause was delivered as he was close enough to get away with it.

So why did Braddon get a number '2' in his conclusion of the total? The answer lay in the method used to communicate the numbers. I will explain what went wrong in a moment.

Back in the Changi POW camp both Piddington and Braddon invented their 'Abacus' system. As I described earlier in this book, (page 84), this was a code delivered in a similar way to the 'Grid' but without a 'Grid' mind map. Instead the system used both hands like an 'Abacus'. The operator would be a member of the audience who was seated in the front row, so his hands could be observed easily. On this broadcast it was my Grandfather George Hart. His hands would be relaxed in a natural fashion on the lap, or anywhere in sight. Holding a coat over the lap was also a popular method, as this helped to hide the hands from those sitting in the same row.

The 'Abacus' could deliver all numbers from 'one' through to zero. Numbers would be communicated individually until all the numbers in any total or sequence was known. In the Braddon trick, the first communication began while Sir Herbert Dunnico was busy asking his 'check' question to the lady escort. The judges were each allocated identity numbers. Dunnico was number '1' and Price number '2'. The audience member was number '3'. The allocation of numbers was easy to remember because it shamefully followed the 'class' system of the period. Dunnico was a first class character while Price was second class. The audience member was a third class citizen due to his insignificance or lack of formal identity.

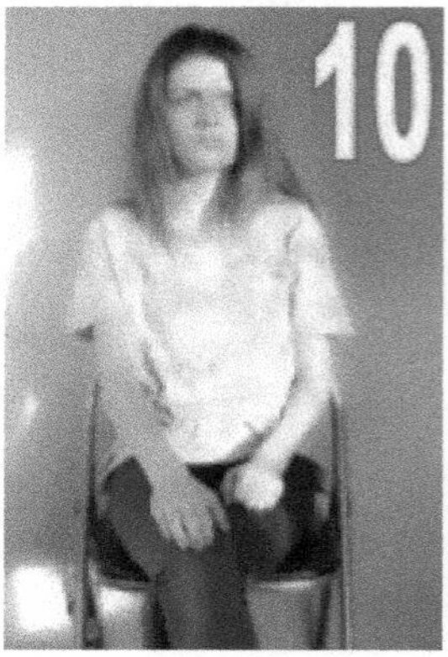

Piddington's Abacus with two hands:

Piddington's Abacus system is a testament to the genius Sydney was. Back in the squalor of the Changi Prisoner of war camp, he and Russell Braddon pitted their minds together to find a method that could communicate numbers covertly. The hands were the obvious answer because they included having the luxury of five fingers that could move. The skill was in the way they used the hands to broadcast any number man could create, whilst the action went undetected even to those looking for such a code. This would be found in the way the fingers and the hands were used, always looking so relaxed rather than hard at work. The name 'Abacus' was given to the system because of the similarity in the manner numbers were created, albeit via a much simpler action. Piddington's Abacus doesn't bother with 'hundreds' 'tens' and 'units' but only single digit numbers with the additional numbers 11, 12 and 13, useful when using the system to show playing card values.

The Two Hand Method:

The left hand is positioned flat on the lap with fingers apart. No fingers are touching the others thus there is a gap between each finger. This represents the number '1'. The right hand is crossed underneath the left or placed out of sight and ignored.

As mentioned the number '1' is represented when all fingers are separated. Bringing any two fingers together while the others remain separated, represents the number

'2', in the same way the beads on the Abacus are collated to create values. Three fingers touching represents the number '3' and the same rule applies for numbers '4' and '5'. The same hand can show the number '6' by creating a natural Fist with the fingers bent under to touch the palm.

Uncross the hands and now the right hand becomes active in showing numbers. To display the number '10' the left hand is in a fist representing number '6' and the right hand flat with four fingers touching to show number '4'. (4 + 6 = 10). The same rule applies to show all numbers up to the value of '11'. (6 + 5 = 11). Both hands fisted represent the number '12' and to show the number '13' both hands come together and interlink the fingers. All the moves are designed to look natural.

The 'Abacus' system can be used in other ways too, for example; to inform of seating positions in the theatre. Row 7 seat number 1 was given in the Murder Game broadcast and the secret assistant's left and right feet were used to indicate if the row was positioned to the left or right of the centre aisle. The foot would simply point left or right while the other foot stood central.

As I mentioned earlier, the 'Abacus' could also be utilised to deliver playing card values, with the 13th card being indicated by bringing both hands together to interlink the fingers or just hold the other in a natural fashion, the hands touching was the idea. Suits would be allocated a number from '1' to '4' and delivered after the value of a card had been given. The value could be communicated in seconds allowing the performer unlimited scope and adaptability within the theme and presentation of a performance. As long as a card was shared with the audience, all kinds of miracles could take place, even while the magician is seemingly blindfolded.

Braddon was back in the studio and while the 'check' question was being asked, secret assistant George Hart communicated the sequence 1 - 2 and 3 to Braddon, thus he now knew that Sir Herbert wrote the first number on the board, Price wrote the second and a member of the audience wrote the third.

What happened next was a miscommunication from the grid operator. George Hart showed the number '1' but Braddon interpreted it as the number '2' when George tried to repeat the number. This was down to the over-play of the natural hand position. The 'Abacus' system requires two fingers to touch when creating the number '2', but the number '1' requires none of the fingers to touch. George moved his hand to close the abacus so he could re-open it to deliver the number '1' again. This move looked like he was delivering the number '2' because George tried to keep the move small. George's fingers may have been showing the number '2' for a moment. Braddon had mistook the number to be a '2' and now there was nothing George could do to rescue the situation without confusing Braddon. This would not have been a good idea on a live broadcast. At this point there was still no code for 'erase last number'. Braddon was still applauded for his near perfect piece of telepathy, which only made the effort look more convincing.

The Colour Challenge:

Sydney Piddington returned to the stage to present the time filling piece using five colours. Listeners had to guess which colour Sydney was transmitting to them through the radio. This filled 3 minutes of airtime and helped keep the show on its 30 minute schedule. Sydney joked after the show that he transmitted the colour pink during the test, a colour not included in the list.

The Tower Broadcast:

It was time to stun the nation with Piddington's brand new book test. Lesley was ready in the Tower of London, still guarded by two very distinguished judges, while Sydney was preparing to begin the book, page and line selection sequence.

Colin Wills announced that this next experiment was the most exciting one, calling it the most difficult test Lesley had ever attempted. Sydney explained to the audience that they would play a part in selecting a page from a number of books with half a dozen people being selected to decide a random page number. This was to exclude any possibility of a pre-arranged choice. He went on to explain that several members of the studio audience would be asked to each write a single figure on a pad of paper and those figures would be added up to indicate the page of a book for Sydney to transmit to Lesley. To leave listeners in no doubt, each figure would be initialled by the person supplying it. He then entered the audience with a pad and a pencil to collect random single digit numbers. The numbers were added together and another member of the audience asked to pre-fix the two-digit total with a number that would put it in the 'hundreds class'. So if the total was 37, and the chosen book had over four hundred pages inside, the prefix number could be 1, 2, 3 or 4 creating a bigger number; for example 337.

A book was chosen by Sir Herbert Dunnico who was asked if he wanted to change his mind. He did change it and he selected a second choice of book. Price and Herbert opened the book at the randomly selected page and added the figures in the page number together to determine which line to use. So if the page number was 337, the line number would be 13 (3+3+7 = 13). In this book the line was;

"...be abandoned as the electrician said that they would have no current..."

Piddington's Most Frightening Blunder:

Interestingly, Sydney became worried when instructing Price and Dunnico to add the figures in the page number together to find a line number. They didn't understand his instruction. Sydney had to physically point to the figures and explain it again. This caused him to become nervous because a miscalculation would ruin everything and there was no code in place to let Lesley know to fail to receive the book line. This was the third show in the series and with another five still to do, a failure of this magnitude could terminate the contract and the end of their fame. The addition total was correct but could they count down to the correct line on the page? Sydney had his doubts and decided he was not going to take any chances. If they had miscounted and read out the wrong line, it would give the game away if Sydney had to correct them. So, as they reached the line indicated by the total, Sydney spoke the words *"I'll just come round and check that"* and approached them to check they had the correct line, to see for himself they had not miscounted the lines down the page and were indeed landing on the line that he required they land upon. Sydney knew that this was a stupid move, and to speak his intentions aloud was even worse as it revealed he was checking on the line, a strange thing to do if this line was to be as random as originally suggested. It took a short while to sink-in but a small group of studio audience members noticed and began to question the move amongst themselves. They had just seen something that was not quite right and Sydney knew it. He asked Dunnico to read the line out loud for the listeners and as he did so, the small group of astute audience members began to understand what they had observed and laughed as Dunnico repeated the line. They had suddenly realised the line was a 'force'. Why would Sydney need to check a randomly chosen line? For what? Spelling mistakes?

Sydney was embarrassed and very concerned. He told them *"be quiet please."* However, the whole scenario began to affect his nerves and his stutter began to worsen, but like a true professional he held things together and continued with the demonstration, using his script as a crutch.

When Sydney was in the Changi POW camp he developed nerves-of-steel. Avoiding being caught running the secret radio required such resolve. There were some close calls and hiding his fears, thus not to encourage a suspicious enquiry, had become a developed skill.

Despite Sydney being shaken through his need to check the line was correct, not a single listener of the radio show realised that something strange had just occurred. The critics also missed it, all the scientists ignored it and no one ever mentioned it afterwards, to the sheer amazement and joy of the Piddingtons.

The line was written up on the blackboard for the audience to see. Once all of this was done, contact was made with the Tower of London. Colin Wills spoke with judge Captain Taprell Dorling who described where in the Tower they were standing, in the stone wall chamber close to the picture of Sir Walter Raleigh, and next to the copy of Sir Walter Raleigh's book 'The History of the World'.

Colin Wills then asked if Lesley was there and on hearing this she said *"yes I'm here, very closely guarded by Captain Dorling and Mr Ross Williamsom. I must say, I'm really glad I've got them here with me"*. Colin Wills then summarised events thus far...

"So far", he announced, "a book has been selected and a page and a line in it indicated by figures supplied by the studio audience. Sir Herbert Dunnico has read the line to the listening audience and at this moment, Dennis Price has just completed writing it on the blackboard in the studio. Now here is Piddington speaking in the Piccadilly studio to ask a question of the judges who are with Lesley in the Tower."

Sydney's voice is then heard as he speaks with the judges to ask some 'check' questions. He asks *"Judge number one, Captain Dorling; has Lesley been with you since she left this studio before the broadcast began?"*

The Captain replies "Yes, every second!"

Sydney continues, *"And Mr Ross Williamson, have you any idea of the book selected, the page number or what the line is?"*

Williamson replies "No idea at all!"

Sydney continues *"In just a moment, at the sound of the gong, I want your complete silence, your sympathy and your cooperation. Now concentrate on the line as I attempt to try and transmit it to Lesley."*

The gong is sounded and all goes silent. Lesley is then heard receiving ideas from Sydney's thoughts, unpicking the ideas to conclude which words make up the line. Lesley speaks the words, 'Men' and 'Electricians' and as if on cue, the sound of a fog horn is heard from a boat on the river Thames. The horn sounded in short and long bursts which gave the impression a Morse code was being used to inform Lesley of the line in the book.

Eventually she says; *"I think the whole line is; 'abandoned as the electricians said there would not be current...' "* Sydney asked Sir Herbert Dunnico to confirm her answer was substantially correct. He confirmed that she was correct and Colin Wills closed the programme.

The book test had worked and Sydney was relieved that all went according to plan. He was also keen to see if the witnesses to his error were letting-on their discoveries with others, but it seemed they had stopped conferring over it. While he was breathing easier in the Piccadilly studio, Lesley and the two judges were enjoying a free tour of the Tower.

It was unfortunate that the boat on the Thames sounded its fog horn at that moment because it was believed by many to be a code. Despite the fact Lesley had spoken the word 'electricians' before the horn sounded, listeners and critics alike concluded this was how the trick was done. This saddened Sydney because he had worked so hard to create a baffling piece of magic. He thought the show was a disaster. However, many, to the relief of Sydney, dismissed the fog horn as being any part of the demonstration, realising such a bold and intrusive method was ridiculous, and continued to be as baffled as they were supposed to be, a fact that Sydney began to realise with the passage of time.

The idea that a written piece of paper was somehow passed to Lesley was now dead in the water, so how was Sydney Piddington able to deliver the line of a freely chosen book, from a randomly selected page, in complete silence several miles away from the studio?

The Method:

For this effect Lesley had to learn 5 separate book lines, all of which were situated on the same page number and line position in each of the five books used. This was easy for Lesley because she was an actress and very used to learning lines and working from cues. Once a book had been chosen, Sydney needed to inform Lesley which book it was. They devised a spoken code to achieve this which was why it was essential that Sydney could be heard by Lesley in this instance.

When Sydney asked the Judges, who were guarding Lesley, the 'check' questions, there was one key-word that signalled which line to deliver. It identified the chosen book and was as follows:

Sydney asked; *"Judge number one, Captain Dorling, has Lesley been with you since she left this studio before the broadcast began?"* The word **'began'** is the key-word and it told Lesley to recite sentence '2' of the 5 sentences she had learned, although they called it sentence 'B'.

If the line to be recited was memorised line '1' then Sydney would have ended the question with the word "Aired". For memorised line '3', he would have ended the question with the word "Commenced" and for memorised line '4' the word "Started" would have been used. Finally for line '5' no end word would have been spoken, the question would just end on the word "broadcast..."

Key-Words to identify which book was chosen...

1 **A**ired

2 **B**egan

3 **C**ommenced

4 **S**tarted

5 – (No word added)

You will notice a simple alphabetical order occurring. There was no natural sounding word beginning with the letter 'D' so the word 'Started' represented fourth position and was easy enough to associate.

Surprisingly, part of this method had already been discovered, before the publication of this book. Shortly after the broadcast, Russell Braddon wrote a letter home to his Mother telling her that "Lesley had learned all the books." The letter was discovered in the Australian State library of Victoria, among Russell Braddon's papers, and it was reported in an article in The National Library Magazine, (Volume 5. Number 1. March 2013), by Nigel Starck, but it failed to get much attention.

The Icing on the Cake Method:

The page and line number were cleverly forced using Sydney's so called 'icing on the cake' method.

Let us say the page number to force was 337. Using a pad and pencil he asked random members of the audience to write a single figure on the pad. As they did so he added up the total in real time, until it was too dangerous to risk another random number. At this point he simply turned to a secret assistant to insert the final single digit, the next figure needed to bring the total to exactly 37. On the Tower broadcast the secret assistant was my great uncle, Dave Daye. Calculating the figures already on the pad, it was easy to add the 'required' number. Sydney asked the same secret assistant to pre-fix the 'hundreds' to create a larger number, thus burrowing deeper into the chosen book.

The process asked the contributors to sign their initials next to the number they had supplied. Although this looked like an official and secure way of ensuring all was true and fair, it really did nothing, meant nothing, and secured nothing. The idea that it removed doubt that all was random was just an illusion. The secret assistant also initialled his contributions and this did nothing to reveal the page number was forced. However, it was a clever deception by Sydney and it worked to help hide the truth for over 65 years.

The small group of witnesses to his earlier error may have gone home questioning the moment, however, it had no overall impact on the show and none went to the media with their suspicions. The good news was that the programme could not be examined because recordings were unavailable to outside bodies, thus no verification of the error could be obtained.

Over the years the moment faded into the forgotten clouds of time, and although the muttering and laughter can still be heard on the broadcast of the show, still no one notices what has really happened. To many it sounds like they are laughing at Sir Herbert Dunnico's delivery of the line, a rude thing to do if it was true, which of course it was not. It was a shame Sir Herbert could never know that?

be abandoned as the electrician said that they would have no current

Sydney accidentally reveals that he is checking to ensure the correct line of text has been selected

"Creativity is allowing yourself to make mistakes. Art is knowing which ones to keep!"

SCOTT ADAMS

Force Page 35

7	**Random**
6	**Random**
8	**Random**
3	**Random**
9	**Random**
2	**Assistant**
= 35	

This system combines both legitimacy and confederacy to deliver forcibility

8 THE FINAL BROADCAST

. . .

Show 8 series 2

By now the Piddingtons were so famous; their tour of Britain's theatres was definite. Their agent and friend Robert Luff had already secured many dates and they would begin almost immediately in Wales.

They had received so many letters from the public over the course of their eight broadcasts that Sydney was in no doubt of which tricks to re-broadcast in this, their final show. The reason for repeating a selection of the demonstrations from past shows was personal. Sydney was troubled by some of the ideas and criticisms people had about his methods. One letter suggested he and Lesley were fitted with Morse code transmitters and receivers that were built into a tooth in their mouths, a rather comical suggestion but exasperating for Sydney, mainly because he imagined people would actually believe it. Any ideas of this kind were viewed as damaging by Sydney because although untrue, it was enough to take the impact and awe away from every demonstration they could perform, on radio and on the stage. Lesley always argued the ideas would never be taken seriously, but Sydney was not convinced. This sort of disagreement was common in their relationship and many conflicts were witnessed by my grandparents. My great uncle Dave once commented to my grandfather George, that the "cracks were quite visible" in their marriage.

For the final show, Sydney wanted to do a demonstration to quash all criticisms and ideas. Where there was a chance he could be accused of using a third party confederate, Sydney would present something that would suppress that idea; same with the idea of a colluding judge, he would invite the most credible of all public figures to judge on behalf of the listening audience.

The script would now include reminders of the obstacles and

conditions the demonstrations faced, such as the fact Lesley was blindfolded with her back to the blackboard and that there was complete silence during the telepathy transmissions.

Finalising this final broadcast together was demanding on the Piddington's, physically and emotionally, causing further cracks in their marriage.

The BBC radio show prior to this involved a book test where Lesley received the line from a book and a member of the public wrote in to suggest Piddington wrote the line on a card in his trouser pocket. This infuriated him because not only was it wrong but believable. He didn't want people thinking his methods were so crude, without imagination, starved of genius and lacking an impressive impact. Sydney knew his methods were amazing, well executed and packed with the talent of a true master conjurer. He felt rather insulted by the accusations of using such basic methods of trickery. Lesley attempted to placate Sydney as he reflected on the criticisms and ideas put forward, however, he found it difficult to put the criticisms aside; it felt personal. Lesley accused him of making her ill as she suffered greatly when he stressed. Sydney reminded her that she always fell ill before a show but this was in reaction to her own nerves not his complaints.

Lesley thought of an idea that she felt would help Sydney diminish his demons. She suggested inviting some of his old POW chums to the final broadcast. Major Osmond Daltry was in London, he had been since their first broadcast, and some of the others were not too far away either. Sydney embraced this idea, a reunion would be a very agreeable way to celebrate the success of the series, say farewell to the radio broadcasts and enjoy the attention and company of those who shared his Changi experiences. He decided he would invite the Major to be a judge on the show, after-all it was he who encouraged him with the idea in the very beginning. This would also allow Sydney a chance to achieve one of his greatest card tricks. He decided he would also invite his Changi mate and pianist Bill Williams onto the show to play piano, thus giving him a boost in his effort to secure some paid musical work.

Bill was an important contributor to the Changi camp entertainment because he made music and that was a gift to all those incarcerated there. He has been forgiven for playing part to annoying the Japs and getting the theatre closed down, but that's another story. Sydney was excited to meet up with him again. He decided to use song choices, including some of Bill's own compositions in two of his demonstrations.

It wasn't long before Sydney, Daltry and Braddon were together again, reminiscing their experiences and working together to decide on acts for a finale to top all finales.

They reminisced about how some of the men in the camp, who were scientists by profession, insisted they conduct their own controlled tests on Piddington and Braddon.

One cynic in Changi was scientist Scott Russell, a man who had accompanied the Shipton expedition to Mount Everest.

When Scott Russell challenged Piddington it was because he was very keen to undertake some experiments to determine the practise true or fake. At the time, and knowing the demonstrations *were* fake, Major Daltry explained to Piddington that because the real object of the tests was about building morale, rather than a belief in telepathy, such investigation would be foolish, and detrimental to their cause. If the demonstrations were proved to be faked, controversy would ease, and the same would apply if they were proved genuine. However, it was decided that the group of scientists made their investigation on the condition that a report was only made public with Piddington's approval.

The tests were carried out over two hours in a prison cell. The scientists supplied their own objects for identification, their own book for the book-test, an obscure technical work owned by one of the researchers. According to Cavalcade Magazine from January 1948, the result of the investigation was published in 1944 and showed an 85% pass rate and the conclusion that no sign of fakery could be found.

Sydney Piddington and Russell Braddon enjoyed much laughter as they remembered the look on their faces as they passed most of their tests. They also recanted how in the Changi camp they had managed to peek at the bundle of objects to be used in the tests and how they managed to use the grid system right under their noses because a blindfold wasn't required. Piddington could sit right opposite Braddon to deliver the 'grid'.

The book test was their favourite ruse because the book was owned by a doctor called Eric Kennedy Cruickshank who was a remarkable man.

Based in a makeshift hospital, surrounded by malnutrition, disease and appalling camp conditions, Cruickshank, 'Shanky' to his mates, managed to maintain detailed patient case notes, often writing on any scraps of paper he could lay his hands on. This experience greatly enhanced his knowledge and interest in nutritional deficiencies and their neurological manifestations. This was the subject of his obscure book

Eric Kennedy Cruickshank

Cartoon of Cruickshank given to him by staff and patients on a ward in Changi POW camp, the artist was Ronald Searle

During the three and a half years spent in Changi (1942-1945) he treated countless cases of Beriberi, Typhus, and commonly found protein deficiency. He was also a good camp 'shrink' and although it was not his true doctorate, he was the one person who understood the importance of maintaining the controversy over the telepathy act, and the one person who would be more than willing to reveal his obscure book to Piddington in advance, which he did. The doctor knew that to reveal the fakery would cause a relapse back into the mental horror Changi, by now, was, and that the minds of the men were desperate for stimulation, conversation and some good old fashioned hope. Such a controversy was great medicine.

On his return to Britain in 1946 he continued his medical studies at Aberdeen University and was awarded a gold medal in 1948 for his MD thesis entitled 'A Clinical Study of Beriberi and the Painful Feet Syndrome'.

To accomplish such an impacting finale, including the most impressive demonstrations to date, whilst also abolishing most, if not all, of the theories and criticisms proposed thus far, Sydney needed the most impressive of all judges. Not just a famous actor or a pretty face but a no nonsense well known and trusted unquestionable character. It had to be the editor of the then respected national weekly publication 'The New Statesman', Basil Kingsley Martin.

The much respected Major Osmond Daltry would be the second judge on the broadcast, a fitting tribute to the man who encouraged him so much in the days of the Changi camp as a distraction from the mental misery and boredom the men were feeling.

The Stubborn Judge:

John Beloff

A respected third Judge, John Beloff, a psychologist, was another figure best known for initiating and nurturing the academic study of parapsychology in Britain.

In 1937, John began training at the Architectural Association in Bedford Square, but he found it profoundly unsatisfying.

While serving in the army during the 2nd World War, he was impressed by JB Rhine's book, Extrasensory Perception, which described painstaking efforts to obtain experimental evidence for psychic functioning.

He was invited to be a fair play judge on the final broadcast of the infamous Piddingtons show. His contribution and status as an investigator of the subject would be a compliment. However as a keen researcher, he insisted that he control the choices, objects and any book lines to be used, thus running the show like a lab experiment, a formula void of any entertainment value and one certainly never to be allowed.

Production manager Piffard refused his request and so Beloff refused to play his part as the third Judge. His planned duties in the show were quickly rerouted to Daltry and Kingsley Martin.

Incidentally, I spoke to John Beloff's daughter Zoe Beloff in 2014 and she told me that her father never believed the Piddingtons had any powers of ESP from the start.

Piddington insisted the final broadcast must include using the separate soundproof studio where he could send thoughts to Lesley from a distance. He wanted to throw a 'curve ball' into the many theories by demonstrating completely silent thought transference, never done before, so spoken code, nor visual cues could be accused. It was a master-stroke by Piddington and one that would baffle the often-opinionated Kingsley Martin who would be sat right next to him as he was transferring his thoughts to Lesley through two brick walls and a padded door. Hoping the 'Statesman' publication would print the story of what its own editor witnessed, real telepathy was the main aim and objective of the trick, especially as this would give a further boost to their up-coming tour. But typically, Sydney Piddington was taking no chances; he had wanted to ensure that no trickery could be accused, therefore, he instructed Kinglsey to handle a brand new packet of playing cards in a manner so no one could see their values, not even Kingsley himself - and only when all was silent and Lesley blindfolded with her back to Piddington, would he then look at the blindly dealt poker-hand of 5 cards, without touching them, and transmit the values to her without a sound.

It was a good idea by Lesley to invite Sydney's Changi mates to the final show. There was a party planned afterwards to celebrate the show and wish them good luck on tour. My Nan Rachel Hart would travel with them and operate the 'grid' and 'abacus' system from the front row or orchestra pit area where she would pose as a prompter. The Prompt Side of the stage in most British Theatres is to the left of the actor, or to the right of the audience. It was a good cover for her and perfect positioning for her task. Nan would also find herself sat with the audience. It all depended on the design of the theatre.

The final broadcast was about to air and over 20 million listeners were sat ready to enjoy, what had become, the talk of the nation. The studio was 'buzzing' with anticipation and curiosity. Sydney called into the audience, *"would anyone like to join us in the soundproof studio to ensure I don't hypnotise Kingsley Martin?"* Many of the audience stood to volunteer and three were chosen to join them.

Commentator Colin Wills was ready with his script in-hand and his big BBC microphone stood tall. Bill Williams was to play-in the show on the piano. All was set for a fantastic finale.

Sydney was secreted in a second soundproof studio with Judge Kingsley Martin and the three keen spectators from the studio audience. Lesley was on the platform blindfolded. Behind her a studio assistant wearing headphones stood poised and ready, at his feet 15 printed cards showing the names of 5 film stars, 5 song titles and the 5 diagrams of the 'Zener' cards, a square, a circle, a star, a cross and the wavy lines.

Production manager, Frederick Piffard started the countdown to open the broadcast, Bill poised to start the theme tune once Fred had spoken his intro line *"ladies and gentlemen we present the Piddingtons"*. Bill Williams rattled his ivories perfectly bringing the theme tune to an end as if he had practised for weeks. *"And once again here is your commentator Collin Wills..."*

The show was on the air and Colin Wills addressed the audience:

"Good evening ladies and gentlemen, here we are at the last broadcast of what must have been one of the most provocative series ever to come on the air. You know it simply as the Piddingtons, but I should like to tell you that when the

Piddingtons first came to this country, the idea was to call the programme 'to make you think!' We didn't call it that but that's what it has done. People have had all sorts of ideas about it, and most of them would admit, I think, that they are still completely baffled. And it's still one of the questions of the day. Well this then is your last opportunity in the present series to decide for yourselves, and to help the Piddingtons tonight they will attempt a number of the tests they have done is previous broadcasts, but with some interesting differences. With us tonight we have in our audience some ex Changi prisoners, who were asked to come tonight to see the show, they last saw, when they and Piddington were fellow prisoners of war in Japanese hands. It's fitting then for me to hand you over now to Major Osmond Daltry, without whose help and encouragement, Piddington's experiments might never have achieved a concrete shape, thus depriving Britain, incidentally, of a very keen controversy. Ladies and gentlemen, Major Osmond Daltry!"

The applause filled the studio space as the Major took to the platform to address the nation. This was only the second time he had broadcast, with the first being on the Piddington's debut broadcast where he told the story of how the act began but had no nerves over it. With a proud face and articulate delivery he directed the listeners to his main point,

"Well I must say that when I first encouraged Sydney Piddington and his friend Russell Braddon to work their early Changi experiments up into a public demonstration, I had no idea that they would lead to such terrifying results as this. I just thought of it as something that would so intrigue our fellow prisoners, that it would help them to forget their unpleasant surroundings. And a Japanese jail is not a place to be recommended as a rest cure. But I had no idea that I was starting something that would end up on the BBC and arouse controversy in practically every home and newspaper in Britain. Anyhow, Ide just like to say, that I think it's a great achievement to have come from those days with the Japanese, not at all a nice race really, to this. And I'm sure you'll all join me when I say, God bless, and all the best for your future Sydney and Lesley Piddington".

The applause complimented his speech and the show began.

The Telepathy Effects:

With Sydney Piddington isolated in a second soundproof studio where no one in the main studio could hear him, surrounded by three audience members and fair-play judge Kingsley Martin, he had fifteen subjects on the table. A choice of five songs, five diagrams and five movie stars.

In the main studio, Lesley Piddington was blindfolded waiting to receive thoughts from Sydney. Kingsley Martin could choose any of the fifteen choices. An attendant, who is the only person who can truly hear what is being chosen through headphones, would hold up a printed placard revealing the choice to the audience - and sound a gong to inform Lesley that Sydney was sending her his thoughts. Lesley would then unpick the thought and correctly identify the choice made.

Judge Kingsley Martin began by choosing the film star John Mills. Lesley identified his choice correctly. Next a member of the audience sitting with them in the second soundproof studio chose a diagram, the square. Again, Lesley correctly identifies the choice. For the third and final part of this demonstration Sydney asks a second audience member, who is with them, to make his choice in silence, only to point at his choice and say nothing. Sydney would then transmit the selection to Lesley in complete silence. The gong sounded ten seconds after Sydney stopped talking and Lesley received the choice of a song. She blindly pointed over to Bill Williams and asked him to play 'On My Return'. He played a few bars of the tune. Lesley was correct and the applause filled the studio.

As agreed to for this broadcast, Colin Wills verified what obstacles faced the demonstrations. He said;

"Well, they've done it again. Two different rooms, a choice of subject by an independent person, no one could possibly have known what that subject was except those in the soundproof studio, and not a word spoken by or to anyone after the choice was made. Well the Piddingtons are certainly hammering nails into the coffin of a great deal of criticism".

According to witness Rachel Hart, ejected Judge John Beloff did not applaud; he sat with his legs crossed and his elbow on his knee, his hand holding up his head from under his chin. Deep in thought, though we don't know for sure, it looked like he was regretting his assertions of earlier, wishing now to be amongst the action, at least for a closer inspection.

The second demonstration on the show was simply to present a list of the five songs on the blackboard and ask Major Daltry to choose two by marking next to them in chalk with a cross.

This was going to be John Beloff's duty in the show, and the original secret method was different to the one finally used to replace it, which actually made Lesley very happy.

The idea was for Lesley to identify the two choices quickly and correctly. This was a swift and smooth demonstration designed to challenge listeners to beat her to the answers. To start the test, Bill Williams was invited to play a few bars from each of the five songs, two of which Bill composed in the Changi camp. This was great recognition for Bill and Piddington's pleasure. The song titles were; 1. '**R**ed Roses', 2. '**O**n My Return', 3. '**F**ar away places', 4. **S**unday in London', 5. '**T**welfth Street Rag'.

Colin Wills verified Lesley is still blindfolded with her back to the blackboard. She identified Daltry's first choice 'Sunday in London' within 8 seconds, and his second choice 'Far Away Places' also in 8 seconds. Due to a last minute change-of-plan, in this test Lesley did not use any help from the 'grid' operator and nor did she need any.

Following this test, Sydney Piddington revealed two letters he had received from theorists. The first comically suggested they used tooth transmitters whereby the tongue could tap out the answers in Morse code. The second suggested the book tests were done by writing the line on a card in Sydney's trouser pocket. Colin Wills confirmed that during the previous week's book test, Sydney's hands were not in his pockets at any time.

The third test required Lesley to be removed from the studio while Kingsley Martin secretly chose a member of the audience for her to psychically find using only thought guidance from Sydney, who would be behind a curtain out of view. The audience member was also asked to choose a number between one and a hundred that Lesley would also identify. The chosen number by a random member of the audience was a new twist on the demonstration, and because it was Kingsley Martin who chose the person, it was definitely accepted to be a fair and true audience member and not a confederate. However, all did not go to plan because a distraction during the set-up process caused Sydney to make a mistake, and although Lesley was successful when revealing the chosen number, she failed to find the person.

Finally Sydney would finish the show with a clever card trick. Again Lesley would be removed while Kingsley Martin was instructed to break the seal on a brand new deck of playing cards. He was told to opened the box, remove the playing cards and take out the jokers and any blank cards. Next he was asked to shuffle them all up and while holding the deck face down, so not even *he* knew what cards were being dealt, deal five cards onto the table, as if he was dealing a poker hand.

All the cards would then be put out of sight before Lesley returned. Still no one had seen the value of the cards. Only after Lesley was returned, blindfolded and all was silent, did Sydney see the value of the cards dealt, not a word was spoken and in that silence Sydney transmitted the five cards to his wife from across the studio. Picking away at his thoughts, Lesley correctly identified all the cards in the poker hand; 7 of clubs, 7 of Diamonds, 8 of clubs, 2 of Diamonds and a Queen of Diamonds.

This was Sydney's 'finale' demonstration and it was impressive. The fact that Kingsley Martin did most of the handling and was definitely NOT a stooge, was a master-stroke because it removed about a million ideas that could be imagined about the method behind this particular demonstration. New deck and no sign of a force. Colin Wills reminded the audience, both in the studio and those at home, the facts of the test conditions. He said;

"Well remind me never to get into a Poker school with you two. I would just like to point out that at no time did Piddington touch the five cards or the pack and that no one knew what the hand was, no one, until after Lesley had been recalled to the platform. And that from then onwards there was complete silence".

The broadcast was then brought to a close by the Piddingtons. Sydney thanked the audience for having them on the BBC and hoped that they found the broadcasts an enjoyment and entertaining whatever else was thought of the act. Lesley added her thanks and mentioned how nice it would be to meet listeners when touring the country. Sydney then reminded everyone that *"there it is, you are the judge".*

The Methods:

So how did Sydney Piddington achieve his first demonstration from the second soundproof studio?

When Kingsley Martin made his choice, the studio attendant held up a printed card to show the audience his choice. Grid operator, Rachel Hart delivered the letters 'Mi' the abbreviation for film star John Mills. The second choice was a shape, one of 5 Zener cards. Here the abacus is used, indicated by crossing the arms over one another and using only the left hand to show a number between one and 5. The 'Square' is represented in the list by the number '4', its correct position in the deck. Rachel showed four fingers together, the thumb separated. The Zener cards number themselves very easily. The circle is made using one line, the cross uses two lines, the wavy lines use three lines, the square needs four lines to make a square shape and the star has five points to it.

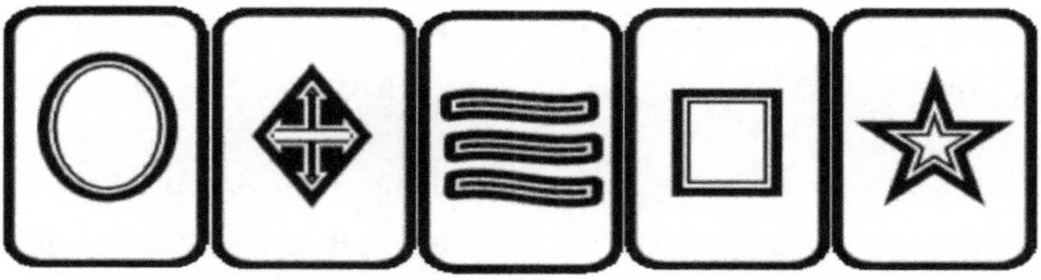

1 2 3 4 5

The hand positions looked so natural they were undetectable unless you knew what to look for. Remember that Sydney only used 5 choices from each category, so it was easier to make dual use of both the 'grid' and 'abacus' systems. For names the 'grid' was used, for diagrams the 'abacus' was used and for a tune the 'abacus' was used while the legs were also crossed. All of the moves were natural and each body position indicated which *mode* of communication was in action and for which set of 5 choices.

For the third choice, one made in complete silence and involving no help from the main studio was a clever twist from Sydney. Dicki Cole was the man who chose the song tune 'On My Return'. Cole was a secret assistant, and in fact a friend of my Grandfather who had moved to the East End of London to work as a black-taxi driver. Earlier Sydney had called into the audience *"would anyone like to join us to ensure I don't hypnotise Kingsley Martin"* and when people stood up, as planned, Dicki Cole did too. Three were chosen and he was one of them, deliberately sneaked into the show posing as a volunteer from the audience.

Kingsley Martin was baffled when Lesley got it right and the story told is one of comedy. As Kingsley Martin watched Dicki point to the song choice without speaking, tapping or any other sound, Kingsley looked convinced this would go wrong and this was shown in his smug smile; he believed there was no chance of Lesley correctly identifying the choice. Sydney pretended to concentrate his thoughts to Lesley through the air while Kingsley observed him. When Lesley was heard to say 'On My Return' his face collapsed into a sudden surprise and disbelief. Dicki almost laughed but held it back until it was safe for him to do so, which wasn't for quite a while. Sydney asked Kingsley to confirm what the choice was. Kingsley replied, rather shaken, *"on my return"*

Bill's Five Tunes:

In the studio printed on the blackboard was the list of Bills five songs. Still blindfolded, Lesley identified the two choices Major Daltry made. She completed this within seconds and without any help from the 'grid'.

Of course, this was due to Major Daltry being more than just a fair-play judge on this broadcast, he was also a secret assistant and he simply picked the two songs they had pre-arranged. If Beloff had participated, the abacus would have been deployed using the 'memory sentence;' "**R**ide **O**ver **F**or **S**ome **T**ea". *(Memory Sentence explained on page 122).* But it was Sydney's incredible card trick that would really utilise Daltry's position in the show.

However before this Sydney demonstrated the parlour game challenge, where a secretly chosen member of the audience is found by Lesley using only her sixth sense, but with an added twist.

The Blunder:

Lesley was removed from the studio and guarded to ensure she could not see or hear what was happening in the studio. Kingsley Martin chose a lady for Lesley to find. The lady would also choose a number between one and a hundred that Lesley also needed to identify. The usual method behind the effect was using the 'abacus' system to show Lesley the row number and seat position. The foot would point left or right to indicate which side of the centre aisle the numbers referred to. However, the 'grid' operator relied upon Sydney verifying the row and seat number before he hid himself out of sight. This he normally did but on this occasion Colin Wills unexpectedly verified the position instead so Sydney didn't bother to further verify the seat position because this would seem to be too much verification. Expecting Sydney to verify, Rachel Hart failed to completely absorb all of what Colin Wills had said, although she remembered the row was number 4 and the chosen number between one and a hundred was the number '1'. When Lesley returned Rachel showed row '4' on the left side of the aisle but could not recall the seat position was number '2'. She folded her arms to indicate she did not have any more information and Lesley had no choice but to venture off and hope to see a clue in the body language of the chosen person. However, she could not tell who the right person was and made a guess that was wrong. She gave up and asked to be told who the person was. She was stood in row '4' near the person and this was classed as close enough to warrant applause.

Rachel would apologise for this after the broadcast and Sydney said it was his fault for not following his normal routine, albeit it would have seemed rather awkward to do so after Wills had already announced it.

Silent Cards: The Poker Hand:

The final trick, 'The Poker Hand' can be enlightened by the following. Sydney gave Kingsley Martin a new deck of playing cards, still sealed in its packaging. He was instructed to break the seal and open the packet. Next, to remove the jokers and any blank cards. Kingsley Martin could see the deck was a real deck of cards, rather than a trick set, as he broke the packaging and thumbed through to locate any unwanted cards. Next Sydney told him to shuffle up the pack thoroughly and he did so. Finally Kingsley Martin is instructed to hold the deck face down and deal 5 cards onto the table. He does so. Up to this point, no trickery has been engaged, and all is true and fair. Finally it is time to dispose of all the other cards, including the unwanted joker cards. At this point, Kingsley Martin is relieved of the 5 dealt cards by Major Daltry who is told to place the five chosen cards out of sight. Daltry announces that he will put them in his pocket.

Once Lesley was brought back to the stage, blindfolded and placed far away from where Sydney and Daltry stand, and only once Sydney has stopped talking, does Daltry retrieve the cards from his pocket and for the first time shows the 5 cards to Sydney, who in silence transmits their values to Lesley. In fact, when Daltry retrieved the 5 cards from his pocket, they were NOT the same 5 cards that went into his pocket. These were the pre-arranged cards Lesley had memorised before the broadcast began. These pre-arranged cards were blindly dealt in the same way Kingsley Martin handled the new deck, thus to show a pattern similar to that of a newly opened, newly shuffled deck, hence the two number sevens that had not quite been shuffled apart. It was a very clever demonstration by the Piddingtons, and until now no one ever discovered that Daltry was in on the tricks.

The series was over and as the faders went down on the number one Piccadilly studios, the Piddingtons were already shaking hands in thanks with the BBC personnel. Even the unsung heroes of the engineering group came to touch palms with them. For a while the studio was alive with the sense of reunion, social hellos and sincere farewells. Grid operator, Rachel Hart shuffled herself away with all the other audience members, to stay and join the party was a 'no-no' for a secret assistant and another dismal fact about being a confederate, even the 'thanks' is given in secret. Her brother Dave Daye picked her up in his taxi and took her home.

Kingsley Martin was thanked for his contribution but he seemed unhappy. The Piddingtons knew they had baffled him beyond what he expected, but instead of congratulating them he was complaining that his role in the broadcast was limited, controlled even, he could not conduct his own tests upon them. The idea that just maybe it was a great piece of entertainment was far from his mind. The Piddingtons had fooled him and that was as good as 'making a fool *of* him'.

The Piddingtons had a date with Robert Luff that evening. They had agreed to meet around the corner from the studio in Jermyn Street. A well-deserved dinner was on the cards, along with details of the tour. Luff had engaged a tour manager, Harry Malcolm, a man who knew everything necessary to guide, transport and accommodate the Piddingtons on their tour. At this stage in their career, they had already succeeded in all they dreamed; they had no idea that in less than three months, the BBC would be offering them a second series of three more shows.

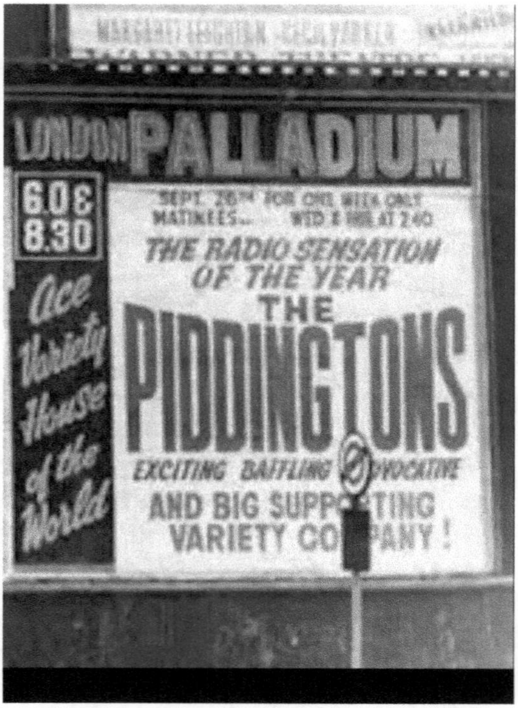

AFTERWORD

. . .

When I look at Piddington's secret methods I see them as innovative, they are without gimmick, the use of modern mobile devices or bespoke props. This was good-old-fashioned manipulation, cunning, boldness and presentation at its very best. Whenever things went wrong, the errors remained invisible and when the illusion of thought transference produced incorrect answers, it only made the idea of ESP more believable. What more does a method need when it covers itself so well, from every angle? Control was always in Piddington's hands, he could steer every effect no matter what would go wrong. Reading the 'grid' was sometimes slow, but this was covered by the idea that sheer concentration was in play. If a line from a book was delivered slightly changed, it was because Piddington was only sending his wife the 'idea' of the line and if Lesley identified a 'brooch' instead of a 'wedding ring', this was accepted as the 'idea' transmitted was of a piece of jewelry. In their theatre shows, Lesley would be sat on a chair on top of a table, and the table surrounded by a circle of people to ensure nothing was secretly handed to her and that everything was seemingly reasonable and above-board. Of course, this put the 'grid' operator in the correct position for signals to be easily read, and for me personally this neatly sums up the genius Sydney Piddington was.

One question still remains; could Piddington's methods still work today? In terms of performance the answer is YES, but with the advancement of technology in magic would his methods be insulted by the existence of such gadgetry? The ability to read the minds of an audience could easily accuse an 'ear-piece' and a success in long distance thought transmission could blame a variety of mobile devices and electronics.

My opinion is the controls introduced by a mentalist using these methods today are of paramount importance. For example; it would seem the Telepath would need to be publicly searched to exclude the idea s/he is concealing an 'ear-piece' or any other device, thus satisfying the techno knowledgeable audiences of today.

I believe Piddington's book-test page-and-line force can still work today, along with his cunning use of secret assistants. His 'objects from the audience collected in an envelope' technique would still baffle audiences today, perhaps more so as sleight-of-hand techniques have greatly improved over the past 70 years.

If Sydney Piddington was alive today, and if he wanted to perform more of his style of mentalism, I am certain he would create a variety of demonstrations designed to evict every methodical accusation thrown at him during his reign as the world's most controversial mentalist. Can you imagine how tangible his 21st century demonstrations would look? I imagine he would stir up as much controversy today as he did back then.

British magician Paul Daniels concludes, if Sydney was alive today, he would still be using these, his acoustic methods and would reject all gadgetry. Sydney knew that his effects could always be achieved without the use of toys. He enjoyed simple but cunningly crafted methods of manipulation, the tactical use of 'time misdirection' and the talents of a wonderful actress.

New branches of magic have appeared over the years and if you look at this progression you will notice that the two person telepathy act has almost vanished. Very few magicians are performing this style of show anymore. The 'Mentalist' has taken over the genre of telepathy and called it 'mind magic' and slowly we have seen the introduction of new demonstrations, such as the ability to read body language in order to discover what a spectator has drawn, written or chosen, thus the two-person telepathy act has evolved into a one-person telepathy act.

With the advancement of communication, the intrusion of social media and video sharing websites the methods behind most of magic is exposed. The idea of a magic circle, originally designed to protect the secrets in magic using a feeling of brotherhood, has morphed into a magic free-for-all, or as I call it, a see-for-all. Audiences know how it's all done and those who don't are not interested or know they can easily find out.

The development of the magic genre is a magical journey in itself, from the days of witches and Merlin to nails up the nose.

In Appendix 1, I discuss the different forms of magic there are. Certainly, when we look at the continuous desire to advance magical effects, improve and reinvent them, we often forget that we also do so because it is a way of rescuing our craft, not just improving it. Perhaps we need to revert back to the old ways, before technology, return to the likes of the Piddington's to awe audiences once again, utilising 'skills' rather than gadgets. It would seem that audiences are becoming desensitised to our many miracles, the 'wow' is dissolving as our magic looks more and more real. Or have they just given up trying to figure us out?

In summary I would simple say; when a man is believed to possess a power that he neither claims is true or false, he is a Manipulatist not a magician. I hope that the world of magic begins to combine the skills of magicians and mentalists to spore more Manipulatists across the world, breeding fresh illusions, events and experiences for the new generations to marvel upon, wonder at, and once again, debate.

Sydney and Lesley Piddington were the strongest Manipulatists of their time and they succeeded in achieving what the rest of us dream about every day, to be the one to rise beyond the magic and be the best and most unfathomable act the world has ever witnessed, and of course for our methods to be impenetrable.

In this personal journey into not just the Piddington's secrets, but also my family history, I realised that I wanted to recreate the two person telepathy act and save it from the dust. I wanted to invent new methods that worked without the need to use a spoken word codes or special devices.

I have worked on it over the past three years and believe I have finally cracked it, methods that work without having to solely rely on a complex 'banter' code, methods that will work at long distance and even in silence.

Inspired by the Piddingtons, I have designed a brand new system of covert communication taking forward what I have learned from the Piddingtons. A system far removed from Piddington's own methods but equally as effective for a modern world.

I hope to be able to teach my methods to those who wish to create a two person telepathy act, bringing the genre back to life in a modern world but with more impact. However, that is my story for another day.

For now, I commend Piddington's Secrets to the world of magic hoping I have contributed something of value on behalf of the Piddingtons and those who needed to know. I hope I have ended the frustration amongst many magicians who admired their work and felt they too wanted to develop the genre.

I conclude my journey and indeed this book in the style of Sydney and Lesly Piddington themselves by saying;

Martin T Hart

"Here is the story behind the Piddingtons and their methods, you may believe it or you may not, but you are the judge"

Martin T Hart

The End

EXCERPTS FROM GEORGE HART'S RAF WRITING PAD

. . .

RAF Writing Pad Front Cover

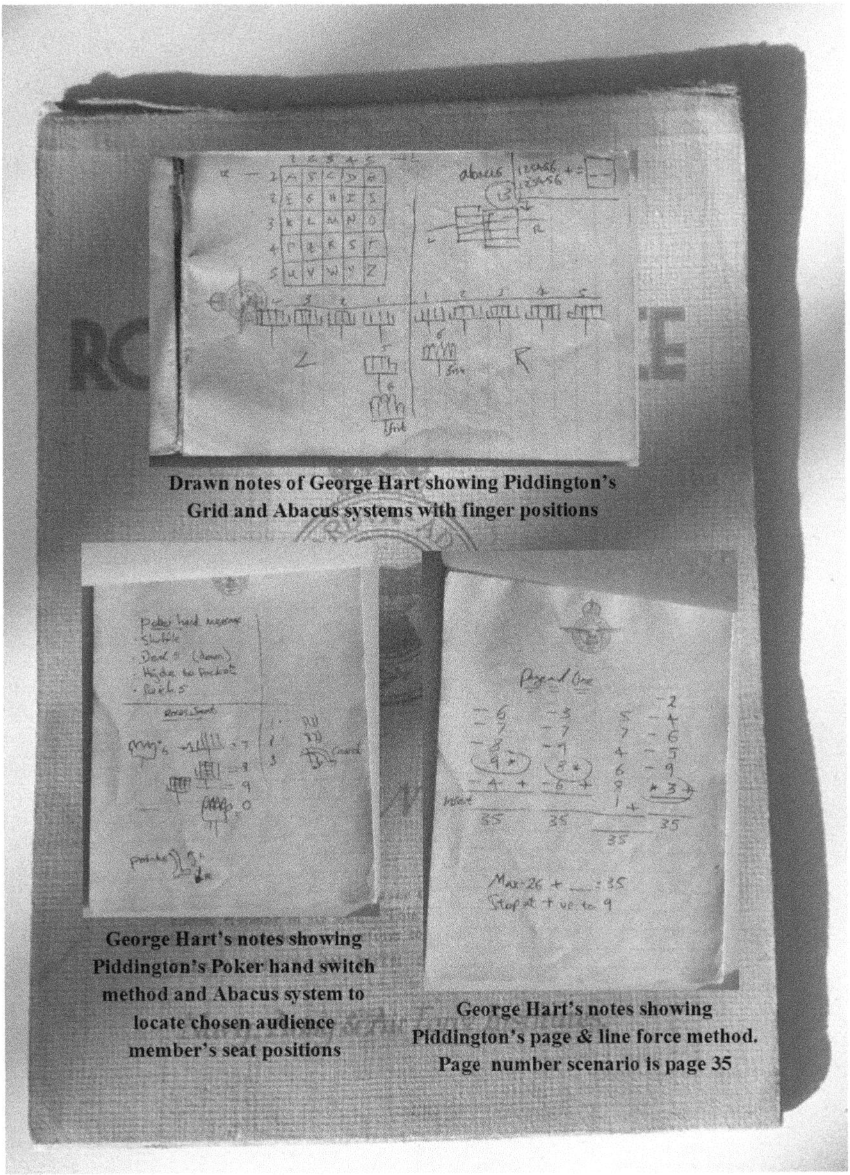

Drawn notes of George Hart showing Piddington's Grid and Abacus systems with finger positions

George Hart's notes showing Piddington's Poker hand switch method and Abacus system to locate chosen audience member's seat positions

George Hart's notes showing Piddington's page & line force method. Page number scenario is page 35

APPENDIX 1. .

A brief look at the progress of magic including how the face of magic has evolved itself from the stage to the streets and through an interesting metamorphic journey of ideas.

We begin with **Stage illusions.** These are performed for larger audiences, typically within a theatre. This type of magic is distinguished by large-scale props, the use of assistants and often exotic animals such as elephants and tigers. Some famous stage illusionists, past and present, include Harry Blackstone, Sr., Howard Thurston, Chung Ling Soo, David Copperfield, Siegfried & Roy, and Harry Blackstone, Jr. Just when audiences got bored with these illusions, the Masked Magician series, written by David John, Don Weiner and Bruce Nash decided there was a new audience waiting for all the secrets behind the magic. Although the methods disclosed in the series were not always accurate, audiences still believed they now knew the secrets. The idea behind the show was to force magicians to invent new tricks using methods that were far removed from the ones exposed.

Platform magic, also known as cabaret magic or stand-up magic, is performed for a smaller and more intimate audience. Nightclub magic and comedy club magic are also examples of this form. The use of small tabletop illusions is common under this genre. The term 'Parlor' magic is sometimes used but is considered by some to be pejorative. This genre includes the skilled manipulation of props such as floating balls, card fans, doves, rabbits, silks, and ropes. Examples of such magicians include Jeff McBride, Penn & Teller, David Abbott, Channing Pollock, Black Herman, and Fred Kaps.

Micro-magic or close-up magic is performed with the audience close to the magician, usually using a small table. This genre is sometimes performed as a one-on-one event. It usually makes use of everyday items as props, such as cards, coins, and seemingly 'impromptu' effects. This genre may also be called "table magic", particularly when performed as dinner entertainment. Ricky Jay and Lee Asher, following in the traditions of Dai Vernon, Slydini, and Max Malini, are considered among the foremost practitioners of close-up magic.

Escapology is the branch of magic that deals with escapes from confinement or restraints. Harry Houdini is a well-known example of an escape artist or escapologist. It is sometimes difficult to name others in this field because the art seems to have died out. However, there are still escapologists out there, such Steve Santini from Canada and Britain's Jonathan Goodwin who combines this art with death avoiding stunts. There are females too, such as Christen Johnson who performs at faith events with her magician husband Kevin Ridgeway under the name Living Illusions and the most famous female escapologist of all, Dorothy Dietrich who performed the first straightjacket escape hanging from a burning rope. She hung upside down 15 stories up without a net.

Mentalism is a branch of magic that demonstrates the performer possesses special powers. He can read thoughts, predict events, and control a person's mind. It can be performed on a stage, in a cabaret, to small close-up groups, or even for just one spectator. Well-known mentalists include Alexander, The Zancigs, Axel Hellstrom, Dunninger, Kreskin, Derren Brown, Guy Bavli and Banachek.

Theatrical séances simulate spiritualistic or mediumistic phenomena for theatrical effect. This genre of stage magic has been misused at times by charlatans pretending to actually be in contact with the dead. Over the years the performance has changed and those who claim to possess true abilities are forced by law to disclaim this when performing, thus introducing the alternative idea that the performance is for entertainment purposes only.

Children's magic is performed for an audience primarily composed of children. It is a wondrous delivery typically performed at birthday parties, preschools, elementary schools, Sunday schools or libraries. This type of magic is usually comedic in nature and involves audience interaction as well as spectator-led effects. There is a big market out there for children's magic and one of the few ways to earn a living performing magic.

Online magic tricks were designed to function on a computer screen. The computer essentially replaces the magician. Some online magic tricks recreate traditional card tricks and require user participation, while others, like Plato's Cursed Triangle, are based on mathematical, geometrical and/or optical illusions. One such online magic trick, called Lady Esmeralda's Crystal Ball, became a viral phenomenon that fooled so many computer users into believing that their computer had special supernatural powers, that a website called Snopes.com dedicated a page to debunking the trick. However, I invite you to witness the illusion first. Just google the name Lady 'Esmeralda's Crystal Ball' and enjoy this cunning piece of misdirection.

Mathemagic is a genre of stage magic that combines magic and the intricate world of mathematics. It is commonly used by children's entertainers and mentalists. I tried to fool British magician Paul Daniels with a piece of 'Mathemagic' back in 1996 but my efforts were so ancient I just looked stupid even trying.

Corporate magic also known as trade-show magic uses our art as a communication and sales tool, as opposed to straightforward entertainment. Corporate magicians may come from a business background and typically present at meetings, conferences and product launches where their patter and illusions enhance an entertaining presentation of the products offered by their corporate sponsors. Pioneer performers in this arena include the late Eddie Tullock and Guy Bavli who you can see in action by searching his name on You Tube.

Gospel magic uses demonstrations of magic to catechize and evangelize. Gospel magic was first used by St. Don Bosco, who was an Italian Roman Catholic Priest, to interest children in 19th century Turin, Italy to come back to school, to accept assistance and to attend church.

Street magic is a form of busking that employs a hybrid of stage magic, platform and close-up magic, usually performed surrounded by the audience. Notable modern street magic performers include Jeff Sheridan, real name Mazio and Gazzo, real name Gary Osborne.

Since the first David Blaine TV special 'Street Magic' aired on our small screens in 1997, the term "street magic" has also come to describe a style of performance in which magicians approach unsuspecting members of the public and perform an effect. Unlike traditional street magic, this is almost purely designed for TV and is focused more on the wild reactions of the public than the trick itself. Magicians of this type include David Blaine and Cyril Takayama.

Bizarre magic uses the mystical, horror, fantasy and other similar themes in performance. Bizarre magic is typically performed in a close-up venue, although some performers have effectively presented it in a stage setting. The late Charles Cameron is generally credited as being the "godfather of bizarre magic." Others, such as the late Tony Andruzzi, real name Tom Palmer, have contributed significantly to its development.

Shock magic is a genre of magic that does what it says on the tin, shocks the audience. Sometimes referred to as "geek magic," it takes its roots from circus sideshows, in which 'freakish' performances were shown to audiences. Common effects include eating razor blades, needle-through-arm, nail hammered into the nose, string through the neck and pen-through the tongue.

Manipulatism. I introduce this for the first time in the world of magic, a new genre from Martin T Hart I call 'Manipulatism'. This is a genre inside which I place myself. The word does not exist but obviously comes from 'manipulate' and 'manipulative'. However, I have decided it should have a meaning in the world of magic that is beyond mere definition and it could be a superb new angle for our industry. "The magician fools the people, but the Manipulatist fools them magician".

Manipulatism is the skill to use the expected and the 'norm' as a tool to produce unfathomable events or effects. For example, using such a skill would allow me to lift the stones of Stonehenge as if they were hollow, even if surrounded by witnesses on site. Another example is drawing pictures in the clouds, using the real clouds in the sky and allowing the spectator to look up and see the result. With the skill of Manipulatism I could openly predict the future and reveal the prediction before the random event even takes place. But the genre is broader than this. Manipulatism could also be used to create beliefs in people that are fictional. This can be used by Police to catch a criminal, encourage incrimination or even confessions. You may say Manipulatism is not new in this regard and you would be right to a degree. A charlatan is a good example of a Manipulatist because he creates an illusion through which to control behaviors, albeit creating a belief by way of lying rather than visual illusion. These are forms of Manipulatism. Sydney Piddington used it too. The ability to openly operate secret moves under the noses of those you wish to fool is Manipulatism at its best, especially of you can keep the secrets undiscovered beyond your own lifetime.

GRID FINGER POSITIONS

GRID - FINGER POSITIONS A - F

. . .

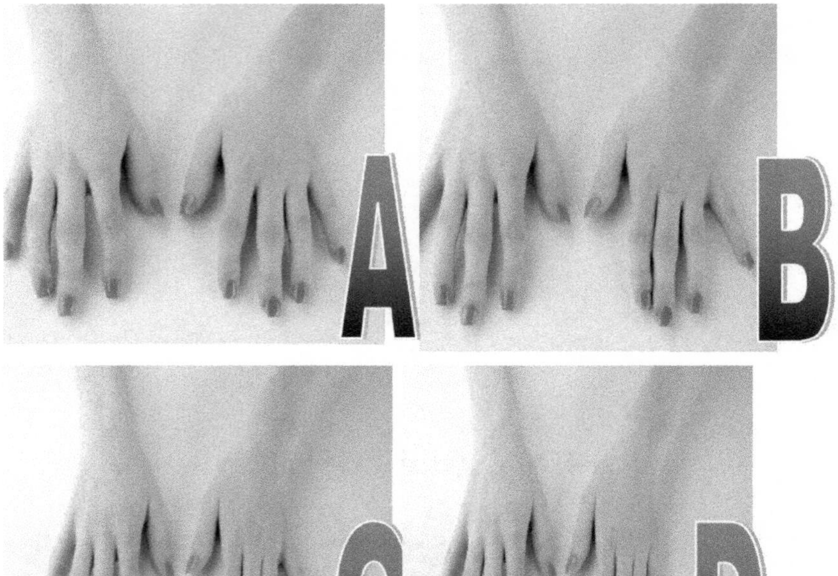

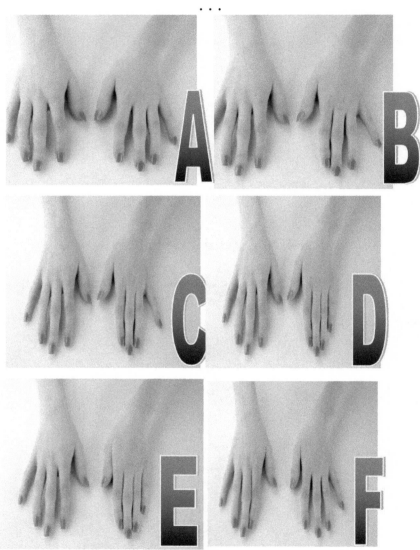

A.1-1 / B.1-2 / C.1-3 / D.1-4 / E.1-5 / F.2-1

GRID - FINGER POSITIONS G - L

. . .

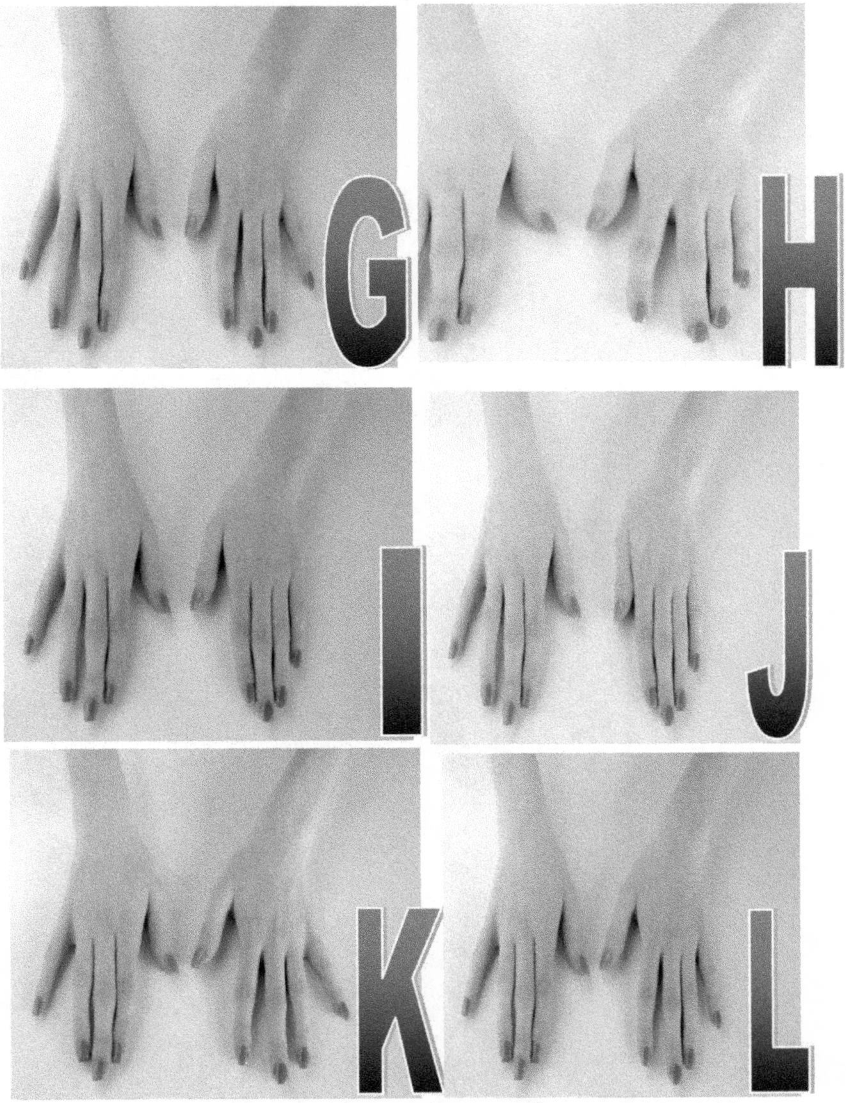

G.2-2 / H.2-3 / I.2-4 / J.2-5 / K.3-1 / L.3-2

GRID - FINGER POSITIONS M - R

. . .

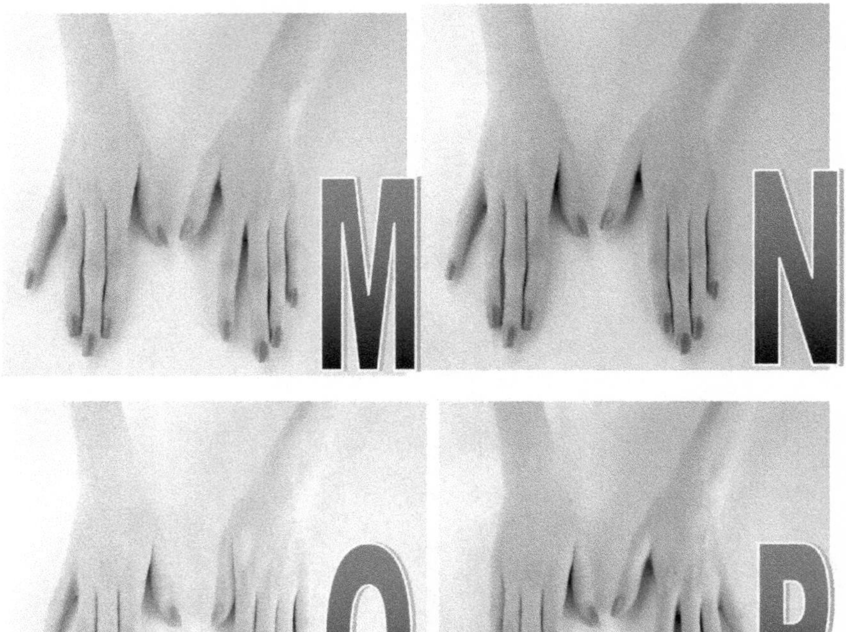

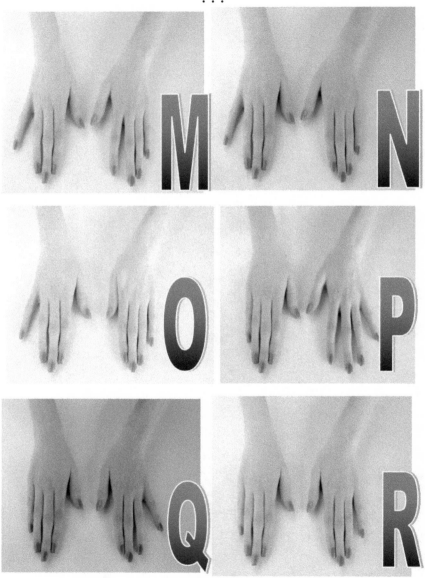

M.3-3 / N.3-4 / O.3-5 / P.4-1 / Q.4-2 / R.4-3

GRID - FINGER POSITIONS S - Y

. . .

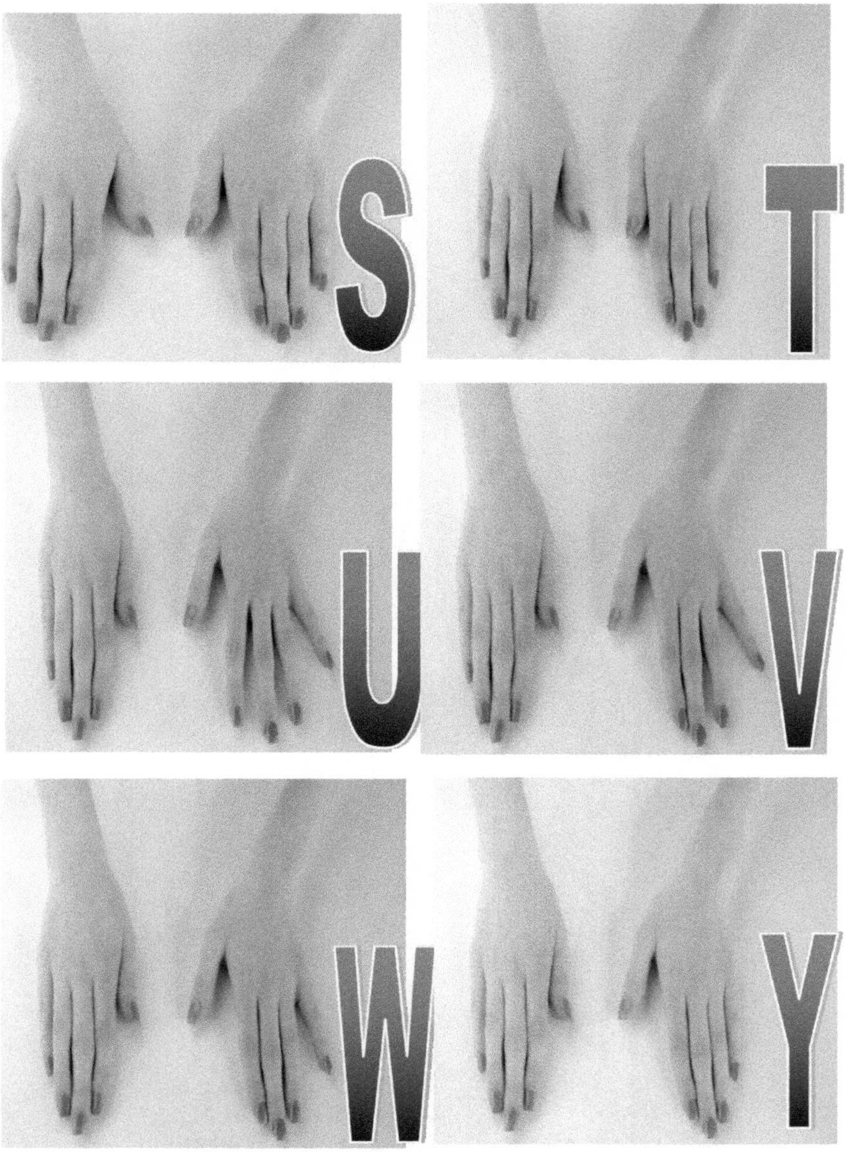

S.4-4 / T.4-5 / U.5-1 / V.5-2 / W.5-3 / Y.5-4

GRID - FINGER POSITIONS – Z

. . .

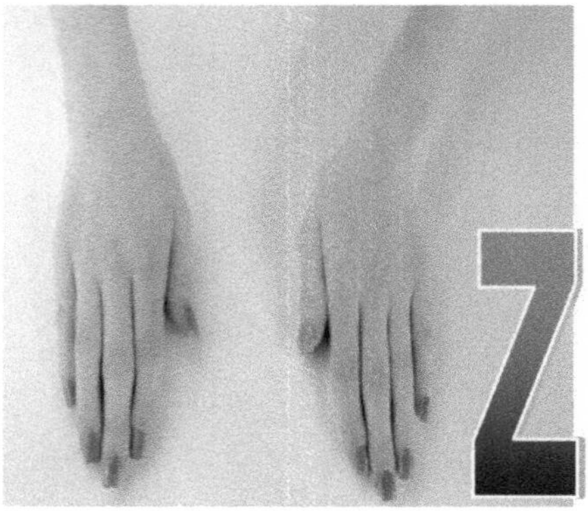

Z.5-5

Piddington's Grid References	1	2	3	4	5
1	A	B	C	D	E
2	F	G	H	I	J
3	K	L	M	N	O
4	P	Q	R	S	T
5	U	V	W	Y	Z

Make this the one book you will
never lend, sell-on or divulge

APPENDIX 2
Alibies by Martin T Hart

. . .

As mentioned in the beginning of the book, here is a sample of my very first magazine puzzle. I hope you enjoy the game and that you can refrain from looking at the answer before solving the puzzle.

To solve the crime and identify the murderer simply spot the only alibi that makes no logical sense according to the facts in the newspaper article. You must be able to explain why the suspect must be lying.

1. Newspaper Report

British celebrity and TV broadcaster Donny Alan was found dead after giving an interview at Radio London to promote his new TV show 'Alan Investigates the Mafia'. Four suspects who were at the studios each had an alibi. Each could say where they were and what they were doing at the time Mr. Alan was murdered. A spokesman from the Mafia said 'don't look at us, we're innocent'.

2. Alibis

Mary the cleaner said: I hated Donny Alan but I could not have killed him. I was in the News Room cleaning up a spillage that occurred after a fight between reporters over a girl.

Laura the producer said. A Member of Parliament had cancelled his interview with the News Programme and although I knew Donny was in the studio next door, I could not have killed him. I was in the stationary cupboard hiding from the news reader.

Sebastian the celebrity magician said. I was preparing for my interview on the Ed Bunny show. I knew Donny was at the studios but I could not have killed him. I was in the make-up department being made-up and dressed for my spot on the show.

Larry the News reader said. I was speaking with a Member of Parliament about an interview. I knew Donny was about to finish his spot on the preceding show but I could not have killed him. I was six offices away from the studios on my desk phone when I heard the gun shot.

ANSWER

***The Answer:** Sebastian the magician could not have been in the make-up department because a radio station doesn't have a make-up department.*

UNFATHOMABLE

A NEW DVD FOR TELEPATHS

. . .

In my efforts to bring back the two person telepathy act for the modern day audience, this title is called "Unfathomable". Here is a new and easy system of covert communication for more modern day telepathy effects that you can perform in silence and at any distance. Perfect for demonstrations on radio and television where your partner is elsewhere. These effects can be performed over the telephone, via video calling or while your partner is completely out of contact with you. NO stooges or secret assistants are needed.

Here is an example: You are having dinner with a friend and you explain that you can communicate with your partner via your thoughts. To prove this you ask your friend to imagine any word, person's name or animal, or if you are feeling very clever, choose a line from any book available. Next you send the thought to your telepathic partner who will then call or text the correct answer to you or your friend's mobile phone. They may also request you stay out of their head as they are busy.

'Unfathomable' is also a collection of new ideas and methods you can use to build, or incorporate into, an unfathomable two person telepathy act, without the need to learn complex word codes or purchase any special devices. This DVD is all you will need to pull off some fresh and unfathomable demonstrations of telepathy.

Look out for this powerful new magic knowhow from 2015

INDEX

• • •

Piddington's Methods Index

Piddington's Judges Index

Piddington's Tricks Index

Other Publications by Martin T Hart in association with MB Global

Unfathomable: 2015

A DVD for the two person ESP act teaching several (brand new) seemingly silent code systems to allow long distance thought transmission effects over the telephone, radio, video calling, even without open contact with a partner during the set-up. Transmit any playing card, any number, any colour and a large variety of other random choice objects. Easily learned. No Complicated codes or systems. No gimmicks to build. No Secret Assistants required.

Next:

Following the publication of this title, Martin T Hart has begun work on his next project, exposing another globally unknown system of methods that have fooled the world to date. To find out more about this exciting new project and more, register for updates at **ManipulatistBooks.Com**.

We Promise:

Your details are NEVER shared with any third parties EVER! We know how to keep a secret!

Lightning Source UK Ltd.
Milton Keynes UK
UKHW010357020522
402333UK00002B/2/J

9 780578 155791